Anzia Yezierska

Twayne's United States Authors Series

Kenneth Eble, Editor
University of Utah

TUSAS 424

ANZIA YEZIERSKA

The picture, created from a 1920 sketch and a 1925 photograph, is published with permission of Flavia Bacarella.

Anzia Yezierska

By Carol B. Schoen

Herbert H. Lehman College,
City University of New York

Twayne Publishers • *Boston*

Anzia Yezierska

Carol B. Schoen

Copyright © 1982 by G. K. Hall & Company
Published by Twayne Publishers
A Division of G. K. Hall & Company
70 Lincoln Street
Boston, Massachusetts 02111

Book Production by Marne B. Sultz

Book Design by Barbara Anderson

Printed on permanent/durable acid-free
paper and bound in the United States of
America.

Library of Congress Cataloging in Publication Data

Schoen, Carol B.
   Anzia Yezierska.

   (Twayne's United States authors series ; TUSAS
424)
      Bibliography: p. 136
      Includes index.
      1. Yezierska, Anzia, 1883–1970 —Criticism
and interpretation. I. Title II. Series.
PS3547.E95Z88   813'.52   81-24080
ISBN 0-8057-7358-4   AACR2

To my mother

Contents

About the Author

Born in Plainfield, New Jersey, in 1926, Professor Schoen was educated in local schools and received the B.A. from Radcliffe College in 1948. In 1961, she resumed her education at Columbia University, receiving the M.A. in 1963 and the Ph.D. in 1968 from the Graduate Faculties in English and Comparative Literature. Since 1968, she has taught at Lehman College, City University of New York, in the English and Academic Skills/Seek Departments. She is one of the coauthors of *The Writing Experience,* published in 1979 by Little, Brown. In addition, she has given adult education courses and published several papers on Jewish-American writers.

Preface

Most studies of writers from minority groups tend to focus on the influence of the ethnic heritage from which the authors spring. Such studies are valuable not only because they help readers understand the culture and ideals which inform the fictions, but also because they focus on the ways various groups have enriched American life and literature. In studying Anzia Yezierska, such consideration is vital, for her East European Jewish background provided a substructure of values and attitudes that determined, in part, her view of life. As the daughter of a devout Hebrew scholar, she was familiar with the concepts and practices of Orthodox Judaism. Her response to her heritage was ambivalent, but whether she was lauding its virtues or condemning its restrictiveness, she was continually reacting to its pressures.

On the other hand, insufficient attention has been paid to the force of American philosophy and literature on writers from ethnic minorities. In Yezierska's case this influence was of paramount importance. As an educated woman who read widely, she knew the works of such major American figures as Emerson, Whitman, and James. Her interest in their approach to life was probably heightened by her association with John Dewey. As a scholar, a teacher, and a friend, Dewey aided Yezierska at a critical point in her career. But even without this stimulus, Yezierska was seriously concerned with the American stress on individualism and the dichotomy between the nation's ideals and its actual practice.

In assessing Yezierska's importance as a writer, it is tempting to overrate her achievement. Despite her extraordinary skill in telling a story, in creating vivid characters in a few, swift strokes, and in suggesting a depth of emotion, she seldom reached the heights to which she strove. Her early work, which has received the most attention heretofore, is often marred by poor organization and shallow characterization. But she was a stern self-critic who was able to learn from her own mistakes. Consequently, her later novels, short stories, and narrative essays reveal substantial improvement which deserves notice. In both the early and the later work, however, it is Yezierska's ability to create a strong central character—the young immigrant girl in her early work, and the older woman in the later—that raises her fictions above the average. The power of this figure vivifies her total production and lends it a significance to all those who are concerned with the treatment of women, of Jews, of immigrants, and of the elderly in American fiction.

In preparing this volume I wish to thank the Boston University Library for making the Anzia Yezierska material available to me and Harvard University Library for providing the Houghton Mifflin letters and the Amy Lowell letter. Special thanks are due to Dr. Jo Ann Boydston for her guidance at the start of my research. But I am most grateful to Rabbi Harvey Tattelbaum and Leonard Bernstein, who read the manuscript and offered guidance, and to Anzia Yezierska's daughter, Louise Levitas Henriksen, who generously shared with me much information I could not have obtained in any other way. She allowed me to study her mother's papers, opened her home to me, and was unfailingly sympathetic with my efforts.

Carol B. Schoen

Herbert H. Lehman College
City University of New York

Acknowledgments

All quotations and paraphrases from and of the writing of Anzia Yezierska are used with permission of the copyright owner, Louise Levitas Henriksen.

The letter to Amy Lowell and the correspondence with Houghton Mifflin Company are quoted by permission of the Houghton Library, Harvard University.

Letters from Anzia Yezierska to W. H. Auden and to John Hall Wheelock from the Scribner Records, used with the permission of Charles Scribner's Sons.

Unpublished manuscripts and letters of Anzia Yezierska in the special collections of the Boston University Library are quoted by permission of the Boston University Library.

Chronology

(circa) 1883   Anzia Yezierska born in Plinsk on the Russian-Polish border, precise date unknown.

(circa) 1892   Emigrated with family to New York City, settled on the Lower East Side.

1904   Diploma from Teacher's College, Columbia University, in domestic science.

1911   Married; six months later, marriage annulled. Married to Arnold Levitas in religious ceremony.

1912   Daughter, Louise, born.

1915   Separated from husband, moved to California.

1915   First published story, "The Free Vacation House," in *Forum*.

1917   Met John Dewey.

1917–1918   Attended Dewey's seminar at Columbia University.

1918   Served as translator for research project studying Polish community of Philadelphia. Studied under the guidance of John Dewey, who left in September for a three-year trip to California and the Orient, thus ending their relationship. Yezierska enrolled in writing course at Columbia University Extension classes.

1920   "Fat of the Land," selected best short story of 1919. *Hungry Hearts* published, and three-year movie contract offered by Samuel Goldwyn.

1921   Returned to New York City. Friendship with William Lyons Phelps, Frank Crane, and members of the New York literary scene.

1923   *Salome of the Tenements* and *Children of Loneliness*. Traveled to Europe.

1925   *Breadgivers.*

1926   *Arrogant Beggar.*

1929–1930   Held Zona Gale Fellowship for writers in residence at University of Wisconsin.

1931–1932   Lived in Arlington, Vermont. *All I Could Never Be,* 1932.

1935   Worked with New York unit of Federal Writers Project, WPA. Continued writing for the next fifteen years but unable to find a publisher.

1950   *Red Ribbon on a White Horse.* Interest in her stories revived; wrote book reviews for the *New York Times* during the next four years. Wrote about problems of the aged.

1964   Appearance at Institute for Retired Professionals. New School for Social Research, New York City.

1970   Died, Ontario, California, on November 22, 1970.

Chapter One

The Immigrant Jewish Woman in America

A Jewish immigrant woman who came to maturity in the late nineteenth and early twentieth centuries in America—these words not only identify Anzia Yezierska, the writer, they define the main influences that shaped her life and her work. In a lifetime that spanned about ninety years, she experienced the persecutions of Czarist Russia, the deprivations of life in New York's Jewish ghetto, the desperate struggle to become part of the American world. She achieved sudden, dazzling success, fame, and fortune, only to be plunged back into anonymity and poverty. Like other immigrants she experienced conflicts between her Old World traditions and the new American values. Like many Jews she was caught between her ties to her cultural heritage and her admiration for the American way of life, and as many women have experienced, she felt trapped between the role assigned to her and her desire for freedom and independence. Out of her troubled life she created stories that capture, with passion and intensity, the confusions and conflicts, the strains and traumas that characterized the immigrant Jewish woman's experience in America.

The Immigrant Experience

Yezierska's family came to the United States from a small town near the Russian-Polish border sometime near the beginning of the great wave of immigration at the end of the nineteenth century, driven out by persecution and poverty.[1]

The American Dream. Like most immigrants who came of their own free will to the United States, they were spurred by a dream of America. The idea of America as the New Jerusalem had inspired the early Puritan settlements; the expectation of religious freedom had encouraged the early Quaker and Catholic migrants; the hope of economic security had motivated the midcentury Irish farmers; the belief in American political freedom had lured the German refugees. For all of these groups and others as well, there was a belief in the myth of America as a New World, one in which the evils that beset the Old World no longer existed, where each man was a new Adam, all equally free and all able to create a paradise on earth. This myth achieved credibility in the cities and towns of Europe with reports of friends and kinsmen who wrote back home of their experiences. Since it is likely that only the successful ones would keep in touch (those who failed would probably like to keep their failure a secret), the reports that came back from the United States were generally favorable and often wildly exaggerated. In one of her narratives, "How I Found America," Yezierska mentions some versions of the myth:

In America you can say what you feel—you can voice your thoughts in the open streets without fear of a Cossack.

In America is a home for everybody. The land is your land. . . .

Everybody is with everybody alike, in America. Christians and Jews are brothers together.

An end to worry for bread. An end to the fear of bosses over you. Everybody can do what he wants with his life in America. . . .

Plenty for all. Learning flows free like milk and honey.[2]

The Cruel Reality.   In order to reach this golden land, however, these immigrants endured a long, arduous journey. Yezierska's experiences, as well as those who came to the United States at this time, were probably no different from those described by Mary Antin, another Jewish writer who came at the same time[3]—the long journey across Europe to the port cities, the weeks of cramped living in steerage as they crossed the ocean. Little wonder that when these immigrants landed at New York, their filthy, bedraggled appearance horrified native Americans.[4]

If these immigrants shared a common dream and suffered much the same dismal journey, they also found a cruel reality awaiting them in large urban centers. Instead of streets paved with gold in New York, there were the densely crowded neighborhoods, thick with pushcarts and the noise of haggling; instead of a home for everybody, there were dismal rooms of the "New Law" tenements whose windows looked out on dark airshafts; instead of an end to worry about bread there was the daily struggle to earn enough to pay the rent and buy food. To cope with this need, many Jews brought their work into their homes. Jacob Riis described the effect in his study *How The Other Half Lives:*

> The homes of the Hebrew quarter are his workshops also. You are made fully aware of it before you have travelled the length of a single block in any of these East Side streets, by the whir of a thousand sewing machines, worked at high pressure from earliest dawn till mind and muscle give out together. Every member of the family, from the youngest to the oldest, bears a hand, shut in the qualmy rooms, where meals are cooked and clothing washed and dried besides, the live-long day. It is not unusual to find a dozen persons—men, women and children—at work in a single small room.[5]

The greatest disillusion, perhaps, was the reception which native Americans gave to immigrants in general. Part of the myth of America had been the idea of acceptance of all peoples, of equality of treatment and opportunity. Instead, immigrants in general found discrimination and exclusion. The employment signs that had once read "No Irish Need Apply" were replaced by those that said "No Jews. . . ," but most groups faced rejection of one sort or another. As John Higham put it, "Whatever significance immigration may have in some inclusive or representative way, it has also been a major differentiating force. It has separated those who bear the marks of foreign origin or inheritance from others who do not."[6] This disparity of treatment might be diminished by the surrender of unique ethnic distinctions, the adoption of the customs and mores of the dominant American culture, and the merging with the older population. But this acceptance of the "melting pot" was not always practiced by native Americans. Pennsylvania coal miners denounced the Italian, Hungarian, and Polish labor arriving among them as a degraded servile class. New racial theories denigrated immigrants from Central and Southern Europe as inferior to the "Nordic strain from Northern Europe." The identification of America with Protestantism brought a fear of the large number of Catholics.

The Jewish Religion and the Problems of Adjustment

The East European Attitude. For the new immigrants, then, the ability to integrate into American life seemed to depend then on renouncing the mores and traditions of their heritage. But for the Jews from Eastern Europe such a solution involved a radical change affecting every phase of life. Excluded from the Gentile world in Europe, these people had found their strength in their religion which provided not only a theology but also a complete ordering of daily life. The sacred texts—the five books of Moses, the other writings which constituted the Holy Bible, or the Torah, and the interpretations and commentaries on those texts, called the Talmud—represented the major symbol of their unity as a people and provided the rituals of religious practice, the values by which the people lived and the social structure which expressed those values. The basic Covenant conveyed in the Torah enjoined these people's obedience to 613 basic precepts contained in the text itself and these commandments were further elaborated by additional rules and restrictions contained in the commentaries of the Talmud. All phases of life, including dress, food, and social mores were covered by regulations so that "no realm of life [was] . . . . divorced from the Law embodied in the Holy Books . . . [and] there was no line between the religious and the secular."[7]

The major obligations to which these regulations related were

the duty to study constantly in order to approach the truth; the obligation to establish a family to preserve and increase the number of those dedicated to the service of the true God; and the obligation to observe the myriad social, economic and ritual activities that regulate the relationship between man and God, between man and his fellow man, between man and himself.[8]

In this world the man who devoted his whole life to study and learning was given the highest regard, and to support his pursuit was considered almost as valuable. The man of wealth was not denigrated, but he lacked the status accorded the scholar and his merit in part derived from using his economic resources for the support of good causes. Hence, the concept of charity was given religious significance. The obligation to establish a family placed tremendous importance on marriage and home, and a full set of ritual obligations guaranteed that life there would contribute to the sanctity of the people. Finally there was the obligation to observe the Sabbath and the Holy Days during which no work could be performed and all energy devoted to prayer, study, and enjoyment. Within the Pale, the observance of these duties could be enforced by the community pressures of the shtetls, or small towns, that dotted the area.

The Religious Attitudes of American Jews. These observances are common to all Jews regardless of their country of origin, but the particular circumstances in Eastern Europe accentuated observance to a level quite unknown in other communities. The Jews who lived in the United States before the major influx of the Russian-Polish migration came from countries that had permitted a more open intercourse with the non-Jewish world, and the relatively greater freedom in America encouraged a wide range of accommodation of ritual observance to the needs of an essentially Gentile world. The earliest group, the Sephardic Jews who came to North and South America from Spain and Portugal from the fifteenth century on, had held places of economic and political leadership in Europe, and although Jews faced certain limitations in political and social freedoms in the American colonies, the acceptance they found encouraged them to participate in the general community and to believe that they would become, in a real sense, part of the United States. In Newport, Philadelphia, New York, Charleston, and Savannah, small but significant Jewish communities existed and their members became factors in the social and economic life of these cities. Religious differences were minimized, efforts were made to modernize the traditional service, and inter-marriage was common. The German Jews, the Ashkenazy, who came to the United States primarily in the mid-nineteenth century also had experienced a feeling of acceptance in Europe, and although there were important differences between them and the Sephardim, they shared with them a willingness to relax ritual practice. Large numbers of Sephardic and German Jews maintained their religious identification, but, as the rise of Reform Judaism in this country testifies, they were able to adjust their practice to conform with American life.

Family Background

The Father's Influence. For these American Jews, as well as for the Americans as a whole, the East European Jews were a strange, exotic group. The men in their long caftans wearing skullcaps and earlocks, the women with their wigs, seemed like representatives from the

Middle Ages. And the sheer numbers in which they came threatened to engulf the existing Jewish community.[9] Many of the new immigrants responded to the problem by abandoning the old customs but Yezierska's family was not one of them. Her father was one of those who pursued the life of a scholar, devoting himself to study and prayer, leaving the problems of economic support to others. In the European shtetl he was undoubtedly regarded with special reverence and at least some of his support must have come from the community. Although there is little exact information, he seems to have been a highly intelligent man with a broad knowledge of the Bible and the commentaries, and he was not without interest in contemporary learning, for at some point he taught himself French in order to read literature in that language. But he was fanatically devoted to his tradition and chose to continue his life of prayer and study even after the family came to New York about 1890. The kind of community support for his way of life barely existed in America on an abstract level and not at all in reality. More often than not, he was probably regarded as an idler, and the burden of support for the family fell on his wife and children.[10] At a time when even the wages of small children were necessary to keep families solvent, the loss of the father's earning power must have created immense difficulties.

Yezierska's Conflict. His daughter Anzia, who may have been about ten years old at the time they came to the United States, speaks of the struggle she endured. In an interview she said, "I worked in the sweat-shops, so many of them I have forgotten the number. And I was a laundress and a waitress in restaurants—terrible jobs that stunned me physically."[11] The father's unwavering devotion to the demands of his religion further prevented the family from joining the mainstream of American life. However much Anzia Yezierska resented having to work at such an early age, she seems to have resented more strongly the continuance of her status as an immigrant, as someone separate from the "real America" of the native born. As strong minded as he, as determined to become a "real American" as he was to remain an Old World Jew, she must have equated the minutia of religious practices with all the forces that kept her out. And her insistence that she had a right to live her own life in her own way was perhaps both a rebellion against her father as well as her father's view of a Jewish life. It was not, however, a rebellion against her own sense of being a Jew. She undoubtedly resented the discrimination against Jews in America, and possibly experienced it herself, but she also believed that denying her own cultural background was more destructive than the prejudice she suffered. In an unpublished manuscript she tells of an incident in which the narrator, a Jewish woman possibly modeled on herself, changed her name in order to get a job. She goes on to say, "But I couldn't get away with it. . . . the day I gave up my Jewish name, I ceased to be myself. I ceased to exist. A person who cuts himself off from his people cuts himself off at the roots of his being, he becomes a shell, a cipher, a spiritual suicide."[12] Till the end of her life she retained a love for the Yiddish songs and stories that she must have learned as a child.

Education.   Her path to becoming like other Americans was through education. It was one chosen by many immigrants and it was particularly appropriate for Yezierska. On the one hand, although some Hebraic scholars often scorned secular knowledge, the Jewish respect for learning was easily transferred, and Yezierska could feel that her ambition had some sanction. Then, too, it permitted her to identify with her father, whose own love of learning dominated his life and that of his family. In addition, it would provide the necessary background that could link her with the native born, and it would serve as a substitute for the sacred texts which she, as a woman, was forbidden to study. Whether the story she tells of paying the janitor's child to teach her to read and write English actually happened to her is impossible to verify, but she did attend night school classes and later lived for a time at the Rand School, a Socialist educational institution. At one point she came to the attention of a group of German Jewish women, including a Mrs. Henry Ollesheimer, who aided immigrant girls to obtain an education. With their assistance she was able to enroll in Teachers College of Columbia University in 1901. In 1904 she had earned a certificate that entitled her to teach domestic science.

A Woman's Role

Although being a teacher gave her status, she was, unfortunately, ill-suited for the profession and thoroughly disliked both it and the subject she taught. It may have been that she chose this particular path because it was the most acceptable one for a woman. In this case both Yezierska's Jewish heritage and the American ideal of women's role

combined to create further problems for her. American culture stressed
women's role as wife and mother and, rather than encouraging careers,
emphasized the woman of leisure as the ultimate model, while the
significant numbers of women in the work force were usually ignored.[13] This attitude was reinforced by the Jewish traditions, which
Yezierska must have particularly resented. In that tradition women
were highly honored as wives and mothers, but any movement outside
that sphere was severely restricted. If she had stayed within that
tradition, Yezierska would have found herself consigned to home with a
moral responsibility for maintaining its holy character. She would have
had to follow the myriad of rules and regulations for its management
which, with the burden of child bearing and rearing, was considered so
important and was so time-consuming as to exempt all women from
any responsibility for prayer and study. But since meditating over the
sacred books was regarded as the highest pursuit in life, it only
confirmed women's second-class status. Little wonder that the morning
prayer for men and boys includes the line, "Blessed art Thou, O God,
King of the Universe, who has not made me a woman." And little
wonder that many women besides Yezierska chafed under those limitations. Excluded from the responsibilities of study and prayer, women
were also seated separately in the synagogue and their contact with men
limited so that their presence would not distract men from higher
thoughts. Although attitudes and practices differed over the centuries,
one study of Jewish women has claimed, "It was a rare Jewish sage in
fact who did not view women as frivolous, ignorant beings, performing
vital tasks in the home and endowed with a simple spirituality, but
otherwise regarded as diverting their husbands from their obligations
to study sacred texts."[14] Her worth would be determined by the way
she ran her home, by the status of her father, her husband, and her sons.
It was even believed by some, a belief mentioned by Yezierska, that she
could not go to Heaven except as the wife of some good man.

Since women's lives revolved around home and family, there was no
place in the tradition for an unmarried woman, for the kind of "career
woman" that Yezierska finally became. But this is not to say that
women did not have major economic responsibilities. When there were
difficulties earning a living, it was assumed that the wife would assist
her husband, and should a woman be married to a scholar, the entire

economic responsibility often fell on her shoulders. So, although the woman was under Jewish law a second-class citizen, in day-to-day existence she was frequently the wage earner upon whose strength the family's welfare depended.

Marriage and Family

For a person of Yezierska's temperament, the dilemma was obvious. As the daughter of a scholar she was well aware of the economic difficulties, the misery and poverty this caused women. Yet while this tradition expected her to work to support her father, it denied her the respect she herself might achieve from intellectual activities. The only acceptable escape from her father's dominion was as a wife of another man, but there the same situation would probably also exist. Much as Yezierska wished to avoid the restrictions that women were subject to, she did not totally reject all aspects of a woman's life. Once, when an interviewer asked her what her ambitions had been when she was twenty-one years old, she surprised him by replying, "I wanted love. It seemed to me that a romantic marriage was the most beautiful of all destinies. Love and a husband and children."[15] In 1910 she married an attorney, but a few months later the marriage was annulled. Shortly thereafter, she married again, this time choosing only a religious ceremony to avoid the legal complications that civil divorce might bring. For a few years she attempted to play the role of wife and of mother to the daughter who was born in 1912. An unpublished short story possibly written at this time offers a clue to her mental state. In it she describes the unhappiness of a woman who had once had her own career but now finds herself dependent on a miserly husband and all her time used up in caring for her infant.[16] Whatever personal problems she may have encountered with her husband, she must have found the position of a married woman stultifying. Three years later she moved with her daughter to California, but, unable to support the two of them, she was forced to send the child back East. Throughout her life, however, she maintained close contact with her daughter.

At this point in her life, Yezierska had been influenced most strongly by the fact of her Jewish heritage, her status as immigrant and as a woman. Out of her Jewish heritage she had preserved the love of learning and a fierce sense of justice, but mostly her response to these forces had been one of rejection—a rejection that left her cut off. By her decision to get an education she had cut herself off from her parents; by her effort to have a career she had separated herself from the mass of immigrants; by her refusal to live the usual life of wife and mother, she was cut off from ordinary women. The terrible loneliness she undoubtedly experienced during this period must have been heightened by the confusions and conflicts within herself. Always explosive, totally involved in whatever goal she was pursuing at the moment, she must also have been aware of the loss that her rejection of social convention had brought in its wake.

The loss of a sense of community might not have been so difficult to bear if she could have felt that she had achieved membership in that real American world to which she aspired. She had, of course, managed all the superficial signs of Americanization. She was well educated; she dressed and spoke like the mass of native-born Americans; she wrote flawlessly and well. She had a career as a teacher, and, although she disliked it, it did provide a measure of financial independence. Yet she did not feel herself part of the community of educated Americans.

John Dewey

It was her meeting with John Dewey, the philosopher, and their subsequent relationship that became the turning point in her career.[17] Through this association, she found a mentor who would guide her intellectual development and encourage her aspirations, who would provide sympathetic understanding of her dilemma and emotional support. While the precise nature of the relationship will never be known, the impact of his personality can be seen in Yezierska's life and fiction for many many years. In 1917, Yezierska had been working as a substitute teacher and as the managing housekeeper in a charitable institution, but she wanted to get the credentials to be a full-time teacher. Apparently stymied by the officials at Columbia with whom she was dealing, she decided to enlist Dewey's support because she had heard of his interest in education. With an aggressiveness that characterized her behavior throughout her life, she simply went to his office and asked to speak to him.

Dewey was, at this time, a man in his fifties, a prominent public figure noted as a philosopher, social scientist, and educator. In public he appeared to be thoughtful and dignified, but he was also a warm family man and a helpful supporter of his students. Yezierska was in her middle thirties, and her physical attractiveness—thick red hair, prominent blue eyes, and a creamy complexion—was heightened by the vitality and energy of her personality. "In conversation, vivid words tumble on each other's heels, and her eyes flash," wrote one interviewer just a few years later.[18] The passionate intensity and magnetic charm of the woman apparently intrigued the older scholar. In the fall of 1917 and spring of 1918, she audited his seminar in social and political philosophy, although such practices were not usually permitted at that time. During the following summer, she served as translator for a team of graduate students sent under Dewey's direction to study conditions in the Polish community in Philadelphia. In September 1918, Dewey left on an extended trip that took him finally to China, from which he did not return until 1921. Apparently all significant contact between them had ended by the fall of 1918.

Effect on Dewey. Brief as the relationship was, it had a profound effect on both. For Dewey it became the inspiration for a series of poems whose existence he kept hidden. These poems show his sympathy and encouragement of her efforts to write about her ghetto experiences. They refer to the wide differences between them, to the many ties that bound him to his present life, but also acknowledge the physical attraction he felt. The difference in their ages seemed diminished by his growing love, and the ties he had to his family and work became "iron bands" that prevented him from expressing what he felt, even while he realized his thoughts are all absorbed in her. Much of the poetry is clearly love poems with tone indicating the nature of his feelings. Whether Yezierska saw all of these poems to her cannot be known, but it is certain that she saw two of them, for they were later included in her novels.[19]

Effect on Yezierska. While Dewey's response to Yezierska was that of a man to a woman, she seems to have visualized him in a more ideal fashion. The innumerable portraits in her fiction of a Dewey-like figure exaggerate his age and accentuate his kindly but lofty nature. There are many poignant retellings of a love story between an older man

and a younger woman, but these often have about them the aura of
hero-worship, and even a mention of him as godlike. It is in terms of
her writing that the effect is most obvious. Yezierska had been writing
off and on for a number of years and had even had a story published but
after her association with Dewey her career moved forward with incredible rapidity,[20] and she even claimed at one time that her career began
with the first story published after meeting Dewey.[21] Also important
must have been her growing sense of the place of the immigrant in
America which Dewey's philosophy at the time was developing. He
believed that assimilation into the total American scene by the new
immigrant was consistent with the maintenance of "positive and con-
servative values of native tradition."[22] In a letter to Horace Kallen,
Dewey spoke of an American nation in which the Anglo-Saxon tradition was simply one of a number. "I never did care for the melting pot
metaphor, but genuine assimilation to one another—not to Anglo
saxondom [sic]—seems to be essential to America. That each cultural
section should maintain its distinctive literary and artistic traditions
seems to be most desirable, but in order that it might have more to
contribute to others."[23] Dewey's most quoted statement on the subject
is his famous remark in a speech to the NEA in 1916: "the hyphen in the
hyphenated American must connect, not separate."[24]

Philosophical Influence. Valuable as that position must have
been in encouraging Yezierska to use her own immigrant experience as a
subject matter for her writing, equally important must have been the
interpretation of the Emersonian philosophy which Yezierska probably
had read, but did not necessarily connect to her own life. Dewey's own
philosophy was derived in part from Emerson and Yezierska was known
to have treasured Emerson, although it is not possible to pinpoint the
exact date at which her interest developed. What Dewey could point
out that Yezierska may not have appreciated was the value Emerson
placed on imaginative intuition and his faith in the individual ability to
develop his own modus vivendi. In the essay "Self-Reliance," Emerson
made the personality the key to human existence and encouraged
individuals to rely on their own instincts for human development.[25]

Dewey's philosophy supplied justification for her rejection of religion while maintaining a faith in spiritual values. He de-emphasized
the search for an end or goal in the world process and examined the

process itself.[26] In this approach, religious dogma assumes less importance, and the crucial point is not whether God exists, but the meaning of God in human experience. Progress and man's role in guiding evolution rather than rational belief were emphasized, and the environment assumed greater importance as a factor in human development. Since human nature was tied to the cultural situation, there was hope for social amelioration through education and institutional reform. His measure, like Emerson's, was that both individual and social institutions were judged by their ability to educate the individual to his or her full potential.

How much of this philosophy Yezierska absorbed is difficult to say. She undoubtedly heard some of it during the seminars she attended, and she must have read some of his books, for she was outspoken in her criticism of his language in them.[27] But just as Dewey-like characters recur again and again in her books and lines from his two poems echo in her writing, so these ideas underlie much of her fiction. They were ideas that fit in with her life as she had led it up to then, but having them supported by so important a philosopher gave her the confidence to follow her own intuitions.

The reason for the breakup of the relationship cannot be definitively known, but it may have been due to the different roles each had assigned to the other, he seeing her as a passionate woman, she visualizing him as a hero and a god. It was a subject she would return to over and over again in her fiction. In any case, the one year of close association provided Yezierska with the courage and inspiration to follow her dream of becoming an author, and brought her increased creativity and success. In 1920, her story "The Fat of the Land" was named the best short story of the previous year and a collection of stories was published under the title *Hungry Hearts*. A few months later the movie rights were sold to Goldwyn Studios for $10,000. Yezierska's career had been successfully launched.

The Role of Spokeswoman and Its Conflicts

The conflicts that had plagued her life did not disappear. She was always to find herself torn between her love for her heritage and her resentment at its demands; she would always feel the pull to become part of American life, yet rail at its materialism and hypocrisy; she would always demand her right to be whatever she wanted to be, yet suffer from loneliness when she cut herself off from others. And she would always search for some perfect world of peace and contentment that constantly eluded her. These conflicts would often mar her fiction, tie her to a limited group of characters and situations which she could never relinquish. But at her best they would provide the raw material for a portrait of struggles of an immigrant woman to find a role for herself in America, a portrait of the hurts she endured, the defeated dreams, the loss of the past without a gain of the present. But she also had a sense of herself as a spokeswoman for all the immigrants, the outsiders like herself, and as this vision of the spokeswoman matured, it became the symbol around which her best fiction would focus.

While the decision to become a spokeswoman gave focus and direction to her personal life, it raised many problems for her as a writer that she could only partially solve and which plagued her and limited the achievement she could gain. On one level there was a realization that literature was art—a communication that reached beyond a depiction of reality to achieve a higher quality. This attribute, which Yezierska had difficulty defining, she sometimes called "beauty," which she often confused with superficialities such as fine clothes and furnishings. And the role of spokeswoman would not necessarily rest comfortably with artistic goals. Then, too, if she were to be a spokeswoman, for whom was she to speak? Her original decision to be the voice of the mute generations of suffering immigrants gave power to her protests against the unjust way they were treated, but her defense of this group immediately conflicted with her sense of their narrowness, rigidity, and unattractive character traits. To be a spokeswoman for the more Americanized world would allow her to appreciate the poise, control, elegance, and comfort of their life, but it ran counter to her awareness of their hypocrisy and materialism, as well as their coldness. What message was she to convey? To paint the life of the immigrants solely in terms of suffering would omit their warmth and vitality; yet to portray the values of Americanization would deny the strength of her cultural heritage. And how should this role of spokeswoman be handled? Should the message be conveyed by a character in her fiction, or should she, as author, stand back and let the message come through in the way she presented her situations? She had enough innate talent as a writer to realize that she had to create a believable world inhabited by people complex enough to seem real, but she was too much of a moralist not to be constantly judging that world and its people.

These problems and conflicts are apparent in most of her fictions, but they become most crucial in the creation of the central character, the young immigrant Jewish woman. This figure was her most significant literary achievement; however, this figure never achieved the stature she could have because Yezierska could never resolve her own relationship toward her. Sometimes she existed to serve as recipient of the author's harsh condemnation; sometimes she served as carrier of the author's message, dramatizing the indignities and injustices from which she suffered; most often the two roles were intermingled, vitiating the strength that either one alone might have given. This problem was not simply a technical one, for it derives from the conflicts of the world in which she lived. More deeply it stems from the psychological confusions that made Yezierska insist on her right to be her own person, but also to have no understanding of who it was she wanted to be. To study her career as a writer is to survey her wrestling with these problems.

Chapter Two
Hungry Hearts

The stories and narrative essays included in *Hungry Hearts* were written over a period of four years and reveal Yezierska's struggle to order the conflicting elements in her life and to find a form through which to voice her sense of the yearnings and the protests of the immigrant in America. The quality is uneven, ranging from the awkwardness of "Soap and Water" to the deft control of the prize-winning "Fat of the Land." Despite their flaws, even the slightest of these stories reveal her growing skill in handling themes and images that would recur in later volumes. They contain narrative episodes that would be reworked continuously throughout her life and characters who would reappear in later fiction. Above all, these stories are valuable for the creation of the compelling figure of the young Jewish immigrant woman, a personality so vividly drawn that she would dominate Yezierska's fiction for years to come.

The Problem of Autobiography

The intensity with which Yezierska conceived this character has led many readers to assume that she was identical to the author, and that the stories were, in fact, autobiography. Since Yezierska frequently used the first-person narrator form for her fiction or, alternatively, used the young woman as the sensibility and voice through which the events are recounted, the confusion of author and character is understandable. Certainly, too, Yezierska drew to a large extent on experiences she herself had had, and in many cases her identification with her leading lady was so strong that the sense of autorial detachment is lacking. But to see these stories only as autobiography is to ignore the significant differences between Yezierska and her main character at the time she was created and to miss the achievement that creation represents. Both Yezierska and the woman she created were dynamic, energetic, and passionately involved in whatever they undertook, but while the character was young, uneducated, spoke in broken English, and had little experience with the world outside the ghetto, it must be remembered that Yezierska was at least in her thirties, had been to college, had taught both in New York and California, and was closely involved with John Dewey professionally and personally. Yet it would be equally wrong to draw too definite a line between character and author, for Yezierska's own struggle and personality are mirrored in the fictional woman and the confusion between the two, for Yezierska as well as for the public, would soon lead to numerous problems.

Early Stories

"Soap and Water." The earliest of the stories, "Soap and Water" was, according to Yezierska, the first story she ever wrote focusing on the immigrants' effort to become part of American life.[1] It is extremely slight, barely a sketch. The narrator is a young woman who visits the dean of her college to discover that she will not receive her teaching certificate because of her unkempt personal appearance. The young woman explains to the reader, as she could not to the dean, that she was so busy working in a laundry to earn her tuition—from five to eight in the morning before school, and from six to eleven at night after the college day—that there was no "time for and strength for the 'little niceties' of the well-groomed lady" (166). She also tells of her disappointment with college where instead of the "place where I should find self-expression, and vague, pent-up feelings could live as thoughts and grow as ideas" (168) she discovered only "dull learning from dead books" (169). Nor did it guarantee acceptance; rather she had come up "against the solid wall of the well-fed, well-dressed world—the frigid white-wall of cleanliness" (169). Caught in a vicious circle where the only jobs she could get because of her appearance were the lowest-paying substitute positions, she was never able to save enough money to buy new clothes. Obsessed with indignation, almost defeated by her struggle, she meets a former instructor on the street and by talking with this woman, now a professor, she finds relief which "unbound and freed me and suffused me with light" (177).

The narrator's final words upon leaving the professor, "America! I found America!" (177) provide an inkling of Yezierska's hopes for immigrants like herself. She suggests that it depends in part on contact

with intelligent Americans, a contact unlike the contact with the dean
which opened the story, formal, authoritarian, threatening, but instead, warm, humane, so friendly that she "felt as natural in her
presence as if she were my own sister" (177). Such a friendship approaches a spiritual contact, a communion that rises above the superficial differences between people. The telling of the story is, however, so
thin that the full implication of the meeting can only be inferred. The
professor's attitude accentuates the cruel insensitivity of the Americans
like the dean who simply did not know that bathtubs did not exist in
ghetto tenements at that time, and were unaware of the immigrants'
hypersensitivity to all the superficial elements that separated them from
the American community. Although the elements here are still confused, and little attention is given to letting the readers experience the
events for themselves, a sense is conveyed of the need for communications between people. Yezierska's role as spokeswoman was finding
expression through the main character.

"**The Free Vacation House.**" What was probably Yezierska's
next story focused on problems of the immigrant wife and mother. This
story, "The Free Vacation House," describes a mother's experience in a
country home run by a charity group. Yezierska herself had never
attended a home such as this, but one of her sisters did a number of
times, and it is probable that Yezierska got the specific details from her.
The sister, however, enjoyed some, if not all, of these holidays and
returned on a number of occasions. How different the experience is in
its fictional form! Presented as a monologue, a tired mother of six
children recounts the humiliations she endured. First, an official-
looking lady visits her tenement apartment to question her in minute
detail about her husband's income and her personal affairs. Exasperated,
the narrator cries out, "For why must I tell you all my business? What
difference does it make already if I keep boarders, or if I don't keep
boarders? If Masha had the whooping-cough or Sonya had the measles
. . ." (99). Her exasperation soon gives way to mortification when the
same questions are repeated at the office of the "Social Betterment
Society" where others can overhear her answers, and it continues during
the medical examination where the doctor touches her so gingerly she
feels as if she "had some catching sickness that he was trying not to get

on him" (104). The joy she experiences at seeing blue skies and green grass, and the pleasure of sitting down for the first time in ten years to a meal she did not have to cook, dissipate as the head of the house reads the list of rules which strictly regulate the women's and children's lives, effectively barring them from enjoying the comfortable chairs under the shade trees, from the handsome front rooms and the carpeted steps. Sadly, she realizes that these parts of the house are window dressing to show to the "swell ladies in automobiles" (110) who come to inspect the institution. She stays for two weeks, however, only because she will thereby save on grocery and butcher bills, and will avoid at least one week's washing and ironing, but when she returns to her tenement apartment, she says "so happy and thankful I was I could cry from my thankfulness" (113).

Although the reader is not given the opportunity to experience the events of the story, its ironic twist—that the greatest value the vacation house had was to make the recipients glad to be home—gives the story a measure of power. The most significant advance over the earlier work is in the character of the narrator who comes through as a believable human being intensely proud that she had never accepted charity before, yet desperately struggling with the burden of too many children and not enough money. The small touches—the unwashed dishes, the nagging children—combine to create a touchingly human individual. Here the implied criticism of the Jewish women's experience is balanced by pride in their way of life. For them, the cost of contact with the dominant culture is the destruction of self-respect.

The stories which were published a few years later show growth in her technical skill, but many of the confusions still remain. Two of these deal with the same main character, a young immigrant girl who struggles between desire for love and the urge to make something of her life, between the temptations of material comfort and the search for something higher. Once more, being a Jew, being an immigrant, being a woman, categorize the individual into a second-class position, but here the redeeming values lie unappreciated and unrecognized. Only the courage of the heroine, her faith in herself and in her barely perceived goal, provide a way out of the trap in which she feels she has been imprisoned.

The Immigrant Girl

"**Wings.**" In the story, "Wings," use of contrasting images of light and dark strengthen the theme. When we first meet the young heroine Shenah Pesah, an orphan brought to America by an uncle, she is looking out the basement window of the janitor's apartment through which the bright May sunshine comes only as "a timid ray" (1). Cut off by her poverty from even the social life of the ghetto streets, she longs for love. Just as the brief bit of sunshine enters the room, so sunshine enters her life in the person of John Barnes, a sociology instructor come to study the life of the new immigrants. Intrigued by the young girl, he plans to use her as a specimen in his study, unaware that to Shenah he is a Prince Charming, a "little brightness" sent to her like the sunshine by "the most High" (2). During a trip they take together so that John can introduce the girl to the public library, John is touched by Shenah's joy and embraces her. For him it is an act of casual sympathy; for her it is ecstatic love. Days pass before they meet again and when they do, John apologizes for the kiss, as Shenah stands stunned, unable to comprehend why her moment of joy and love should require an apology. John, realizing that the girl has read more into the kiss than he intended, packs his suitcases and leaves. Alone again in her basement room she mourns briefly, and then as a "solitary ray of sunshine," (34) steals into the room, she defiantly resolves to show him that she can push herself up and tells herself "to show him that you're a person" (34). She realizes that in their brief moment, he has given her something precious, that he has "opened the wings of your soul" (34). The contrast between the darkness of her immigrant life and the light she connects with Barnes is somewhat heavy-handed but an interesting contrast is made between natural light and the artificial lamps of the library, which were "like so many eyes looking you over." (28)

While the emotionalism of both of the main characters in "Wings" is excessive, Yezierska seems to be struggling to give form to her sense that there is a communion between people of which physical love is simply an outward manifestation, and that a higher meeting, even for a brief moment, is the more valuable. This is the knowledge that makes Shenah say that Barnes has given her a precious gift. At the same time Yezierska makes us aware of other precious gifts that Shenah unknowingly possesses, and, in her ignorance, trades away. Her heroine pawns her featherbed, her last remaining treasure from Russia, to buy a garish hat with red cherries on it and a bright green organdy dress—her final link to her past thoughtlessly sacrificed to buy the tawdry superficialities of the New World. In this incident, action and symbolic meaning are perfectly merged.

"Hunger." Shenah's career is followed in a second story, "Hunger," telling how she breaks out of the prisonlike life with her miserly uncle to make her own way in the world "to work myself up for a somebody!" (41). At the first factory where she applies for work, she meets Sam Arkin, who befriends her. His gentleness brings a rush of confidence. Later, when he takes her to a restaurant for dinner, he brags about his bank account and his ability to write his own name. His passionate declaration of love and his willingness to give her all his money tempt her only briefly from her determination to achieve more than material satisfaction in America, to search rather for the essence of the American way of life which she had once imagined to be incarnate in the person of John Barnes. She tells Sam of the hunger she feels. "This fire in me, it's not just the hunger of a woman for a man—it's the hunger of all my people back of me, from all ages, for light, for the life higher." (63). Despite Sam Arkin's melodramatic collapse at the end, the story avoids complete bathos by the same raw courage that marked the end of "Wings," the same yearning for fulfillment to achieve more than a material satisfaction in life. In the inability of Shenah even to articulate precisely what she means, Yezierska has communicated the nature of the dream that is at once the dream of new immigrants and the hope of all young people.

The contrast between Sam Arkin's goal in life and that of Shenah Pesah underlines one of the central confusions that Yezierska, as well as other immigrants, faced in their new lives in America. What was it they wanted from America? On the one hand, the obvious need was for economic security; mired in poverty, the newcomers could see no higher goal than simply amassing sufficient funds to rent a decent apartment, buy good food and clothing. Such is Sam Arkin's approach. But Shenah's goal, however vaguely she expresses it, sees beyond those necessities. For her, the American dream and her Jewish tradition are both influential factors. Devoting oneself to the life of the mind is the most worthy pursuit in the Jewish tradition, and the American dream included the notion that each individual has the right to develop his or her own potential to its fullest extent. However easy it is in theory to separate these two goals—money or the search for higher values—in real life the interrelationships are far more complicated. If an individual has a great love for the potential beauty in life, that person can only be depressed by the ugliness of poverty and long for the beautiful things that only money can buy. And even the most spiritual of scholars needs funds for food and clothes. At times it seems that, in America, money has a spiritual quality and that the possession of beautiful things indicates a beautiful soul. In Yezierska's early stories, the two opposing goals are either so clearly separated, as in "Hunger," that no conflict seems to exist, or so thoroughly confused that their opposition is not apparent. Thus, John Barnes in "Wings" is an image for the fineness in America as much for his elegant tweed suit as for his academic profession.

Stories of Love

"Where Lovers Dream." As Yezierska began to see the complexity of the problem, her stories developed greater depth. But the growth of her understanding did not follow a clear course, and the contrast between two stories of love and marriage reveals how fragile was her understanding. In the first of these, "Where Lovers Dream," it is the material success which seems to have become a sufficient substitute for any higher aim or goal. The plot involves David, a young man studying to be a doctor, and his ghetto sweetheart, Sara, whom he tries to Americanize by buying her copies of the *Ladies Home Journal* and taking her to restaurants to show her proper table manners. When the young man is about to graduate, his wealthy uncle, who has paid for his education, persuades him to find a rich American woman to marry rather than to "waste his love on beggars" (153). Although Sara, who narrates the story, marries someone else and is a mother, she still dreams of her old love and goes to look at the "great stone house" (162) where David lives with his wife. This is one of the least successful of the stories in the book, for the deserted woman's aspiration has no greater significance than the rather banal fact that it is probably better to marry a rich man one loves than a poor man one does not.

"The Miracle." Here Yezierska was able to show the flimsiness of a purely materialistic attitude, but instead of choosing between the two approaches, she concocts a resolution which permits both. Her handling of the images reveals the great technical strides she was making. The narrator, a young girl in a poor village in Poland, longs for love, but the prospects for a dowryless woman like herself are sorry:

In my village, a girl without a dowry was a dead one. The only kind of man that would give a look on a girl without money was a widower with a dozen children, or someone with a hump or on crutches. (114)

When a letter from America is brought to her father to read, the whole village comes to gape over the wonders of the New World, where "millionaires fall in love with the poorest girls . . . where men run after women, and not like in Poland, the women running after the men" (115, 117). To secure passage money for her seems an overwhelming task—the family is so poor they do not even own furniture valuable enough to sell. The only items of worth are the father's Saifer Torah— the holy scroll of the law—and the mother's silver candlesticks, used for the lights on Friday night with which every religious Jewish home welcomes the Sabbath. When the father protests against giving up the sacred text, his son points out that Jewish law permits a man to sell even the Holy Book to help marry a daughter. The mother's response to the idea of selling her candlesticks is poignant: "It's like a piece from my flesh. . . . We grew up with this, you children and I, and my mother and my mother's mother" (122). But the treasured symbols of the tradition are sold, and Sara goes to America.

If the story had ended there, it would have been a tiny gem in which the reader could see and feel the terrible cost that the immigrants paid in coming to America, not simply in material terms, but also in the sacrifice of the traditions—the Holy Law and the Sabbath—which had sustained them through generations of persecution—for a patently false dream of wealth and perfect love. In this segment Yezierska has not found it necessary to underline her thesis; the very choice of details does it for her and she lets them carry the full weight of meaning with marvelous economy. The story, however, continues, detailing Sara's life in America, with its hardships and, of course, its lack of love. A visit to a matchmaker confirms the obvious; the only marriages available to a dowryless woman in America are the same as they were in Poland. But Sara conquers her despair and decides to focus on making a life for herself by going to night school. There she meets her ideal man, a teacher, who, however, finds himself a prisoner of formal education and conventional traditions which prevent him from expressing his emotions freely. As he teaches Sara from his books, so she teaches him from her heart, and in the love they find with each other comes the miracle of the story.

Sara at the end of the story thus has the best of both worlds—economic security and a sense of participating in the higher life of a teacher. Instead of coping with the issues she has raised, Yezierska has simply avoided them. There is no doubt that she was dealing with one of the most difficult problems in the American dream, the American value system, one that had vexed and would continue to vex writers with broader backgrounds than hers, so it is not surprising that she could find no really adequate resolution within the confines of the short story. Perhaps she made her fullest statement in the choice of her title, "The Miracle," indicating either that such a marriage can occur only in the magic land of America, where miracles are possible, or possibly she is saying that such a union is a miracle at any time or any place, even in America.

The solution for the women in these two stories was through marriage, suggesting that Yezierska accepted the idea that a woman's fulfillment, her sense of being a person could not be achieved without it. It was a position fully in keeping with her Jewish heritage. At the same time she was also developing another kind of fulfillment for herself—that of spokeswoman. In these early stories the main character serves as the voice through which Yezierska criticized the injustices in both the ghetto and the American worlds. The approach is often too simple to support the moral purpose, but the unity of the author's message and heroine's personality make a strong and vivid statement.

Stories of Artist Figures

"The Lost Beautifulness." Yezierska, in her wish to be a writer was aware of the fact that another purpose of literature was the creation of beauty. This artistic function served her moral purposes, but it also involved a different range of values. In these early stories the search for beauty is often confused with material well-being or in achieving equality with Americans, but in two of them the heroines are quite specifically designated as kinds of artists. They find their expression in very different forms, yet for both there are obstacles that block achievement. Hannah Hayyah in "The Lost Beautifulness" is only a laundress, but she is able to express her love of beauty even in the simple act of ironing clothes. As Mrs. Preston, Hannah's employer, says, admiring the loving care with which the woman does her work, "You are an artist—an artist laundress. . . . An artist so filled with love for the beautiful that he has to express it in some way. You express it in your washing just as a painter paints it in a picture" (76). But Hannah wants beauty for herself, and Yezierska shows with bitter irony how this attempt produces brutal consequences. Hannah has struggled for years to save enough money to have a "white-painted kitchen" exactly like the one in the home of the rich woman she works for. When she finally achieves her dream in time for her son's return from the army, she invites all the neighbors in to see it. The landlord, however, realizing that she has improved the apartment, raises the rent. Unable to pay the increase, the family is evicted, and as the son comes up the street he finds his family with all their household goods huddled on the sidewalk. The definition of the artist here is close to the concept that Emerson had expressed when he said all of man's creations are works of art, and Hannah's desire to express herself was like the flowing forth that Emerson had characterized as the creative spirit. While one theme of the story is the condemnation of the current economic system, it also dramatizes the struggle between an artist and a money-hungry world. It is a struggle which here the artist can only lose, and this creative spirit turns in on itself with destructive consequences.

   "My Own People."   The second story is more obviously concerned with an artist, in this case a writer, and once again the Emersonian dictum that art is found in the ordinary acts of life provides the underlying structure. Here, however, so many extraneous elements are included that they befog the central theme.[2] The main character in "My Own People" is Sophie, a young woman who has chosen to ignore her family and move into a furnished room by herself in order to secure the peace and quiet she feels she needs to become a writer. But instead of becoming productive, she finds that her "words failed to catch the life-beat—had failed to register the passion she had poured into them"

(229). When after weeks of struggle she finally begins to write the way she wants to, her talkative landlady interrupts her. Unable to get rid of the woman, Sophie watches her free time melt away. Just as Sophie is about to ask the woman to leave, the woman's daughter comes in to say that she has been forced to leave the factory because she is under the legal working age. The child's news sends the landlady into tears and stormy invective against the inspector, the system and even the president:

The president from America should only come to my bitter heart. Let him go fighting himself with the pushcarts how to get the eating a penny cheaper. Let him try to feed his children on the money the charities give me and we'd see if he wouldn't better send his littlest ones to the shop better than to let them starve before his eyes! (235)

When the younger children come home from school pleading for something to eat, Hannah turns her passionate outburst against them, "Gluttons—wolves—thieves. . . . I should only live to bury you all in one day" (237), but her words have no effect on them.

Into this storm of rage comes another tenant, Shmendrik, an old man noted for his learning and saintly disposition, to invite the group to share a box of cake and wine he has received. All the anger and sorrow disappear in the dizzying joy of this special treat. At the height of the feast the representative of the charities, the "friendly visitor," enters unannounced and decides that they no longer need the funds they have been receiving. Sophie, who has changed during the story from dislike of Hannah's clamorous emotionalism to admiration for her ability to savor every moment of life, screams angrily at the intruder. Her words go unheeded, but the experience has taught the young girl to realize that her own labored writing was too rational, too far away from the spontaneity of life. When she returns to her room, she finds a story of Hannah which almost writes itself, for she now has a theme and a subject: "It's not me—it's their cries—my own people—crying in me! Hannah Breineh, Shmendrik, they will not be stilled in me, till all America stops to listen" (248).

The number of different problems which Yezierska was trying to cover in this one short story was far too great and the effect is to blur the significance of any particular one. Not only is she striking out at the economic system—the unexpected ill-effects of the child-labor laws and the cruelties of the philanthropies—but she is also trying to depict the immigrant mother's problems and those of a man who remained true to Old World values. With so many distractions, the central issue of the artist finding the material and the form of her expression is confused. Yet the working out of this theme represents a significant advance for Yezierska, for here the yearning to be "a person," the vague ambition of Shenah Pesah, has found a particular meaning and the burden of the "blind, aching feeling" of the narrator in "Soap and Water" has found a voice. Both the heroines in these two stories have a sense of their need for creativity in life. In both of the stories the same anger at their poverty-stricken circumstances continues, but both of them have found a way to express the potential of life, a form to communicate their sense of the meaning of life and of its possible beauty. The melodrama in the ending of "The Lost Beautifulness" and the confusing number of themes in "My Own People" limit the effectiveness of both the stories, but Yezierska had found her path.

Major Achievements

"**How I Found America.**"   That path was clearly demarcated in "How I Found America," which Yezierska was working on just before the book was published. It is one of the most frequently anthologized of her works, and it represents just such a clear statement of her themes. The confusion between economic goals and spiritual ones is transcended and an explanation is provided to show how the economic deprivation which the immigrants experienced came to represent the failure of the American dream. It also presents a person, in the character of the narrator, who embodies in concrete terms the frustrating experiences and slowly clarified dreams of one immigrant woman. The first part of the story covers the narrator's life from her childhood in Russia until she and her family land in America. It opens with the scene of the father teaching the neighborhood children in a one-room mud hut, while the young ten-year-old girl who is telling the story watches for the Cossacks who would close the school down for violating the law. When the class is dismissed for dinner, the girl, fearing that she will be cheated out of her potato, deserts her post, only to have the Cossacks come unawares. The children scatter, the school is closed, and the family's livelihood destroyed. But a glimmer of hope appears when the villagers bring a letter to the father to read. The letter tells of the immense wealth to be made in America—$2.00, the equivalent of 4 rubles—in just one day, that white bread and meat are eaten every day in rooms with doors, and best of all, that "there is no Czar in America" (256). The family decides to emigrate.

Part II of the tale recounts the misery the young girl found in the ghetto of New York. Instead of a golden land, she sees "narrow streets of squeezed-in stores and houses, ragged clothes, dirty bedding oozing out of the windows, ash-cans and garbage cans cluttering the sidewalks" (263). And as she looks at the sunless rooms of her new home she wonders, Where is America? Where is the land of her dreams? Instead of education, she finds herself in a factory, half-maddened by the "merciless grind of the pounding machines" (266). When the boss announces that he is cutting their wages, the young girl, aroused by the injustice of the action, confronts the owner. Her reward is, of course, being fired. Inspired by her dream of doing something more than manual labor, she rejects an opportunity to attend a vocational school.

Part III shows how the girl moves from despair to new hope. She is still sure that "Until America can release the heart as well as train the hand of the immigrant, he would forever remain driven back upon himself, corroded by the very richness of the unused gifts within his soul" (283). But she does not see how that could happen for her. When her family is evicted for nonpayment of rent, the girl is forced to go back to the factory to help support them, submitting now to her discouraging fate, but keeping alive the spirit of courage and faith that she will somehow "dig my way up to the light" (287). Hoping that education will provide a solution, she attends school, but she is discouraged by the traditional curriculum. Only when she meets her sister's teacher does she sense what it was she was looking for, longing for—an American who cared to listen to her story. As the teacher reads a passage from Waldo Frank, the girl realizes that all Americans—immigrants and native born—share in the creation of America and that with a friend to talk to, she, too, can participate in the search, that the search itself which she has been carrying on all that time is what she has been looking for—"the soul—the spirit of America" (297).

In this telling, the personality of the narrator is almost completely submerged in the events she tells, and the telling itself is handled with such economy that the tale assumes a mythic quality. It becomes the legend not just for one immigrant girl, but for all immigrant women; and not just for immigrants alone, but for every woman growing up, seeking to leave her own enclosed world and become part of the larger world around her. It captures the warmth, but also guilt, connected with home, the brutal indifference of the outside world, and the despair that almost destroys courage and will. But it insists that the long road can be successfully traversed with the help of a friendly mentor.

The form of the story is also a great improvement over the previous versions. The three-part breakdown carefully isolates each step of the journey, allowing its particular meaning to come through without the need of elaborate explanations by the author. The incidents, especially in Part I, swiftly sketched yet completed with key detail, capture Yezierska's passionate intensity, which is not superimposed on the incidents, but an integral part of them. It is most valuable, however, in the fact that it suggests more clearly than previous immigrant writers what it was that newcomers wanted from America, why the mere acquisition of wealth would leave a David Levinsky in Cahan's novel, *The Rise of David Levinsky,* [3] still vaguely unfulfilled, the awareness that beyond the satisfaction of material needs, however vital these may have been, there remained a deeper need, a longing to find the America of golden ideas as well as gold. It showed why the horror of poverty, even though it might have been less severe than the world from which they came, so destroyed the refugees, for it represented not just a continuing economic struggle which generations of struggle had taught them to cope with, but a defeat of the dream itself, that there was a world where people might not continually exploit one another.

"The Fat of the Land."   Equally popular as an anthology piece and probably the best story in the collection is "The Fat of the Land," the story that brought Yezierska her first recognition. Published in 1919, it won for its author the O. Henry Award as the best short story of the year. It uses elements that had appeared in earlier stories, but here the emphasis lay not on the yearning for a higher life, but the consequences of a life that was never touched by any of that spiritual beauty. Through the character of Hannah Breineh, Yezierska traces the rise of a family from the poverty of Hester Street to the affluence of Riverside Drive, only to discover at the end that the hollowness at the center of

life had become an abyss of despair. When the story opens we see
Hannah Breineh as a struggling wife and mother, cursing angrily at her
life as the evidences of poverty dominate the scene—the leaky wash-
boiler, the soap-box "refrigerator" on the window sill, the screaming
baby, broken stove and unmade bed. While she and a neighbor, Mrs.
Pelz, reminisce about feasts in the Old Country, Hannah's baby topples
from his highchair. Instantly her tone switches to frantic terror. "He's
killed! He's killed! My only child! My precious lamb!" (182). For the
rest of the section Hannah's moods move in the same pattern of elation
to despair at a dizzying pace. She alternately curses her children for their
unending desires she cannot fulfill or wails hysterically at the thought
they may be hurt. As one neighbor says while watching Hannah, "Such
a mouth! With one breath she blesses him when he is lost, and with the
other breath she curses him when he is found" (196).

The three scenes that follow detail Hannah's rise. The first, many
years later, shows Hannah now ensconsed in a brownstone on 84th
Street, entertaining her old neighbor. Amazed at the signs of wealth—
"shades on all the windows like by millionaires" (196), steam heat, rich
carpeting—Mrs. Pelz can only pull her shawl more tightly around her
to hide her ragged clothes. As the two old friends gossip in the kitchen,
however, the emptiness of Hannah's life becomes apparent. Unlike in
Delancey Street, where everyone knew everyone else, the neighbors
uptown do not care "if the person next door is dying or going crazy from
loneliness" (198). The servants prevent Hannah from using her own
kitchen; the children, although they have become successful, ignore or
are ashamed of their mother's Old World ways. The next scene, a dinner
party in honor of one of her sons, poignantly shows the gulf that lay
between Hannah's world and that of her children. As they banter
among themselves discussing the fact that the President is coming to
see her son's play that evening, Hannah cries out, "What worth is an
old mother to American children? The President is coming tonight to
the theater, and none of you asked me to go" (207). In the final scene,
Hannah is living in an apartment hotel on Riverside Drive. Deprived
now even of a kitchen, she lives in "an empty desert of enforced
idleness" (210) and finds eating in the restaurant a humiliating experience because of her lack of table manners. In a fit of rebellion she goes
back to her old neighborhood where she joyfully bargains with a

fish-peddler, only to discover when she returns to her elegant residence that the doorman will not let her carry her packages up the passenger elevator. After a fight with her daughter over the mother's ghetto ways, Hannah storms out of the apartment back to her old neighbor, Mrs. Pelz, who still lives on the Lower East Side. There she gives vent to the anger at her children.

Why should my children shame themselves from me? From where did they get the stuff to work themselves up in the air. . . . It is I and my mother and my mother's mother and my father and my father's father who had such a black life in Poland. . . . It is our choked thoughts and feelings that are flaming up in my children and making them great in America. And yet they shame themselves from me! (219)

Hannah spends the night in her friend's apartment only to discover the most unpleasant truth of all—accustomed to good mattresses, warm blankets, and cleanliness, she can no longer endure the cold, the mice, the foul odors of the ghetto. She does not fit into the new world of her children, but she has also lost the old world of the ghetto: "She had outgrown her past by the habits of years of physical comforts, and these material comforts that she could no longer do without choked and crushed the life within her" (222–23). With bitter laughter, she stands in front of her Riverside Drive home and mutters, "The fat of the land. . . . the fat of the land" (223).

The irony of the tale is made the more piercing because the main character is so vividly rendered. Based on reminiscences of her own mother, Hannah Breineh, with her intense, overemotional responses as a young mother, her nervous fear and angry snarls at the servants, her pent-up rage at her children's regarding her as an embarrassing remnant of a past they want to forget, looms over all the events and characters in the story. At the end, as she realizes that she is trapped in gilded isolation, she assumes a kind of tragic grandeur. Yezierska had caught the sheer energy, the sense that, in spite of incredible work and worry and striving, some part of life had never been lived, and that while Hannah Breineh may experience the emptiness, she will never understand the why of it—all these qualities move the tale beyond mere storytelling into the realm of "felt experience."

Analysis

In all these stories Yezierska had caught some of the contradictions
and confusions of the Jewish immigrants, and of immigrants in general. For these people the old traditions were at once an imprisoning
factor that separated them from the American world, and at the same
time provided an honored value system that gave substance and meaning to life. For these people the dream of America had been cruelly
exaggerated, and the economic and social deprivations they suffered
were not only difficult to endure in and of themselves, but also brought
with them discouragement and despair as evidence of the failure of that
dream. By focusing on women, Yezierska caught the particular harsh-
ness they faced. The wives and mothers, caught in the same economic
struggle and lack of social status they had endured in the old country,
now were trapped by the American world, which seemed bent on
destroying their self-respect. In the characterization of the young
immigrant woman, however, Yezierska had begun to forge a new path.
Battling the forces that would trap her in traditional molds, she still
preserved many of the values of that tradition—the love of learning, the
belief in the life of the spirit, the sense of moral indignation at social
injustice. For her the American myth of individual self-fulfillment was
something she would fight to achieve with little more than raw courage
to aid her. She fought against the pull that was both back and down,
and the indifference, insensitivity, and distaste of the American world
that prevented her from moving forward. But for this young woman
there was also the potential reward of contact, however fleeting, with
the America of myth. Most important of all was the development of the
vague yearning for creative expression, into a sense of mission that
joined the artist's urge to give form and order, beauty and meaning to
experience, with a protest against injustice. The artistic urge found a
focus in the vision of the writer as a spokeswoman—the voice that could
give expression to all the inarticulate sufferers in their midst. And it
was from those brief moments of contact with America that her
vocation was developed.

In her tales of artists, Yezierska stressed the fact that the acceptance of
that vocation brought with it extreme sacrifices, not simply in a
physical lack, but in a sense of isolation. Even when she is walking by

the teeming streets of the ghetto, working in crowded factories, she is separated by her own awareness of the unexplored possibilities of life. She is an observer of, rather than participant in, the worlds through which she travels, even an observer of herself. Her urge to find a role makes her a figure for the artist who, despite frustration, remains faithful to a vision for which she is willing to deny the ordinary standards of responsibility to cling to a higher morality. In these stories Yezierska was moving toward the creation of a *persona,* a fictional *I,* to carry her message of struggles and meager pleasures which had been largely ignored in the American literature. Yezierska seems to have most deeply wished to have that story receive its due. To say that she had almost the sense of being a prophet is perhaps to overstate the case, but that captures the fervor with which Yezierska undertook her mission. She saw herself as the epitome of all working-class immigrant women, suffering, mute, whose very existence remained unrecognized, as if they were invisible. It was this quality that both intrigued and dismayed the critics who reviewed the book.

Critical Reception

As Edward O. O'Brien, the editor who selected "Fat of The Land" for the O'Henry Prize in 1918, said at a later time, "Anzia Yezierska voices the smouldering idealism of the Jewish immigrant in a vibrant and nervous idiom which tends to rhetoric and false sentiment. Miss Yezierska has real power which needs greater restraint to make a more effective impression."[4] And most of the reviews of this book tended to agree. One called it "Fierce and savage and to our sober self-control almost unreasonable in this cry for beauty, life and freedom that rings from the heart of this oppressed race in the voice of one of their number."[5] The reviewer in the *Dial* commented that "Miss Yezierska has a firm command over her subject matter; when she restrains herself, she is artistic, but her impassioned writing is thin and sentimental."[6] In *Bookman,* however, the reviewer approved of the style and wrote that "No more powerful indictment of certain phases of the immigrant problem could have been penned. Miss Yezierska's idiom is excellent. It would be a pity if she turned to a more polished formula."[7] In the *Nation* the reviewer felt that her little book is "full of tears that sometimes come too quickly," but at the same time he added, "And yet she has struck one or two notes that our literature can never again be without and she deserves the high credit of being one of the earliest to put those notes into engaging fiction."[8] Samuel Raphaelson in the *New York Tribune* noted that some of the themes were trite, but added that "This book is worth reading for the tang of the minor characters."[9] The *New York Times* reviewer said that "It would be difficult to point to a group of short stories within the covers of a book that make a stronger appeal to all that is best in the human heart."[10]

Despite these generally favorable reviews, the book did not sell well. Yezierska's letters to her publisher were full of advice on how to market it, but they did not seem to help. Yezierska's life at this point must have been in a turmoil. The turn of events that followed brought such a startling change that it seemed the very stuff of fiction itself.

Chapter Three

Confusion and Compromise

Hollywood and the "Sweatshop Cinderella"

Looking back at the years of Yezierska's first success, it is hard not to believe the Hollywood publicity releases that came out when *Hungry Hearts* was sold to the movies—the sweatshop Cinderella suddenly discovered by the world, transformed from total anonymity into a prominent figure, from extreme poverty to glamour and wealth, a mute, downtrodden working woman magically given a voice and an audience. But such sensational headlines were not only misleading, they masked the real struggle that Yezierska endured, the perseverance and even audacity that marked her progress to recognition, and, finally, the very real conflicts that success brought in its wake. More important, such an approach ignores the artistic skill which she had developed over long years of hard work.

The period between the publication of *Hungry Hearts* and the sale of the movie rights was particularly difficult for Yezierska. John Dewey had already left for Peking, signaling the end of any possible contact between the two. Despite the initial interest of the reviewers, occasional interviews, and readings, the sales of the book were disappointing, and the lack of a larger public acceptance and her precarious economic situation were discouraging.[1] Even allowing for her exaggerated emotionalism, a letter to Amy Lowell written at this time indicates her state of mind:

I live alone in a little room like a prisoner in a cell. I never meet anyone to talk out what's aching in my heart. If you would only let me come to you sometimes and take my hand in yours it would be new life to my stifling spirit. And I feel I could bring to you new life—the life of dumb, unvoiced worlds.[2]

But if Yezierska was despondent, she was not willing to accept her state passively. Her letters to the publishers were filled with specific ideas for the advertising and distribution of her book, followed by angry charges when she felt they had not been accepted.[3] When she decided they would not help publicize her book, she took matters into her own hands and literally stormed into the office of Frank Crane, a former minister who was then a leading columnist for the Hearst newspaper chain. In the article he wrote the next day, he describes his experience:

I got a new slant on America from Anzia Yezierska. She walked into my office one day and brought the Old World with her. She had not said three words before I saw farther into the heart of Russia and Poland than I had ever been able to do by reading many heavy books. She was Poland. She was the whole turgid stream of European immigration pouring into our home country. The waters of the stream laved my consciousness.[4]

Captivated by this passionate, dynamic woman, he repeated her message to the world:

Here was an East Side Jewess that had struggled and suffered in the desperate battle for life amid the swarms of New York. She had lived on next to nothing at times. She had hungered and strived and endured. Why? Because she wanted to—write. . . . From a sweatshop worker to a famous writer! All because she dipped her pen in her heart.[5]

It was Crane's column which was brought to Goldwyn's attention and led to his decision to buy the movie rights. On 17 December 1920, Yezierska wrote her publishers telling of Goldwyn's offer of $10,000 plus $10,000 per year for three years.[6] Later that month she wrote of negotiations with Fox Studios as well and finally that the contract with Goldwyn had been signed.[7] It was an event that was to transform Yezierska's life, but it was one that occurred as much because of her own actions as the vagaries of fate or luck. By 28 January 1921, she was ensconced in her office in Hollywood.

The publicity campaign conducted by the studio capitalized on the myth, suggested by the reviewers and by Crane, of her as an ignorant sweatshop worker. It was an image which Yezierska herself had encouraged even before she went to Hollywood. In an interview published in *Good Housekeeping* in June 1920, she had glossed over all the details of her life since 1901, giving the impression that she had only recently emerged from the factories on the Lower East Side.[8] But the conflict between the image and the reality created a dilemma. The perpetuation of the myth brought her a great deal of attention, national publicity, and introductions to a literary community. The writers that she speaks of meeting in Hollywood, such as Gertrude Atherton and Alice Duer Miller, were not the most serious of the period, but they did offer an opportunity for discussion of art that she seems to have constantly yearned for. And, of course, the financial rewards of Hollywood were beyond her wildest dreams. On the other hand, the maintenance of this image meant a denial of her true self, a sense of flying under false colors. And it denied the seriousness of her intention to be not only a popular writer, but also an artist as well, a creator of a fictional truth more significant than the truth possible in autobiographic reminiscences. The image of spokeswoman was confused between the two roles.

This conflict was but one of many that plagued her during her period in Hollywood. The writers she met were more interested in discussing the size of their fees than questions of literary style. For them it was, as she later quoted Will Rogers as saying, an opportunity to "lap up the cream while the going's good."[9] They were not horrified, as she was, when the film studios tampered with their scripts. But when Goldwyn hired Montagu Glass, a well-known Yiddish comedy writer, to add bits of humor to her material instead of concentrating on the story of suffering and struggle that she had envisaged, her sense of artistic integrity was truly offended. She was further disturbed by the gulf she saw widening between herself and the poor people with whom she had always identified. Her sense of Jewish values, which were usually voiced in her fiction by rabbinical figures patterned after her father, consistently equated goodness with the denial of material possessions. How could she justify her own enjoyment of wealth?

All of these conflicts exacerbated what was the most serious problem—her inability to write during this period. She described her method of creating in an interview published in 1922 as "striving painfully and longfully over the least of her stories, passionately seeking and intrinsically finding, rejecting all that is trumpery and

false."[10] In practical terms, this meant that every piece was the product
of numerous revisions and total rewritings. A study of her unfinished
manuscripts shows a method of composition that she probably followed
all her life. Basically, it involved rewriting each story completely a
number of times, beginning each time as if for the first time. There
might be four or five versions of the same short story with varying sets
of incidents usually clustered around a central image. In addition, each
version was revised heavily to sharpen the portraits and heighten the
drama.[11] Such a process was time-consuming to say the least. And it
was further complicated by her insecurity in criticizing her own work:
"What shall I keep, and what shall I throw away? Which is madness,
and which is inspiration? I never know. I never know whether the
thoughts I've discarded are not perhaps better than the thoughts I've
kept?"[12]

And with all the publicity generated by the Hollywood press agents,
she was under considerable pressure to produce. Houghton Mifflin
urged her to finish a novel; there were offers for serial rights, for weekly
columns, for stories and articles. In April 1921, she returned to New
York, but as early as February she had written of her plans to leave
Hollywood. A letter dated June 13 was written on Goldwyn stationery
suggesting that she had returned to California. This personal restlessness seems to have mirrored her inner confusions, which were in turn
reflected in the two books she published in this period—the novel
Salome and the collection of short stories and narrative essays entitled
Children of Loneliness. Both were erratic in quality, containing much
that should have been thought through more carefully, but also revealing flashes of honesty and freshness of vision that had always redeemed
her work. In both, the figure of the immigrant woman dominates the
scene, and in the creation of this figure, Yezierska showed growing
confusion as to her message and her missions.

Salome of the Tenements

When the manuscript of the novel was sent to Houghton Mifflin in
the fall of 1921, it was not well received. The editor wrote to Yezierska,
"The book is not an entire success. . . . You have not succeeded in
making Walling [Manning] a convincing person. . . . and Sonya is

done with power. . . . but repellent."[13] In a few months she wrote to Houghton Mifflin on the stationery of Boni and Livright, indicating that she had found a new publisher.[14]

This first novel must have dismayed both the reviewers and its potential readers, for it seemed deliberately set out to attack the very audience to which it might have appealed. As if in reaction to the Hollywood myth about herself as a Cinderella, Yezierska created an antimyth which rejected the sentimentalized vision of the poor but virtuous immigrant girl who captivates and marries the kind American millionaire and lives happily ever after. It is revised to show the scheming duplicity of a heroine who used every trick she could think of to trap a wealthy husband, only to find that, unlike in the fairy tales, they will not automatically live happily ever after, but, more likely, end up in the divorce courts. At the same time Yezierska retained many stereotypes that accentuated the less attractive aspects of Jewish immigrants so there was, in effect, something in the book to offend everyone.

Source of the Plot. The outlines of the story were based on true events—not autobiography, but the life of an old friend, Rose Pastor Stokes. She had met James Phelps Graham Stokes while he was living and working at a settlement house sponsored by his family on the Lower East Side and had married him in 1905. The wedding received much publicity in the New York press, which emphasized the unusual nature of the liaison.[15] Although both the Gentile millionaire and his Jewish immigrant bride were interested in Socialist causes, the tie was not sufficient to keep the marriage going. Rose Pastor Stokes became well known as "Rose of the Ghetto," a spokeswoman for radical causes, and during World War I she was arrested and tried for making speeches against American participation in the conflict.[16] At the time of her trial, it was evident that she was no longer with her husband and that they had been "just friends" for many years. They were finally divorced in 1925. Mrs. Stokes was also a talented artist and a dress designer.

In translating the story from fact to fiction, Yezierska omitted all the political implications. By this omission, she withdrew any social justification for her heroine's actions and forced the reader to concentrate on her personal motives. Also left out were all of Stokes's social and feminist concerns—her efforts to help organize labor, to spread knowledge of birth control, and to revise divorce laws to permit women greater equality in the courts. Instead, Yezierska concentrated on the artistic side of her friend's character, thus emphasizing the special role of the artist in society. These changes point up Yezierska's intentions in writing this fiction and emphasize once more the fact that it is literature and neither autobiography nor biography that was her focus.

The Legend of Salome and Contemporary Retellings. Another indication of Yezierska's intentions was the transformation of her friend's personality into a literary creation befitting the legend that had inspired the title. Much of the confusion about this novel could be resolved by reference to the story of Salome—the beautiful girl who demanded the head of a saint as a reward for her voluptuous dancing. The story had received considerable attention when Oscar Wilde retold a version of it in a suppressed volume.[17] Wilde's version, a character study in abnormal psychology, became the inspiration for Richard Strauss's intense and emotionally charged opera. Its first New York production in 1905 roused a storm of protest and a later planned production in Boston was prevented. Yezierska's use, which can be gleaned from the frequent mentions of Salome in her novel, visualizes the heroine as so driven by passion that she does not care how she gets her man, whether dead or alive. For her the figure of John the Baptist is that of a "high-souled saint" who loved "with a self-destruction, the white fleshed loveliness of Salome."[18] Thus the images of power, lust, and destruction are the basic foundations of the novel. Yezierska seemed to be writing a response to those who rhapsodized over the "rags to riches" story of the immigrant and sentimentalized the unpleasant facts about ghetto poverty and life in general. Antiheroes and antiheroines had begun to find a place in American literature in the writings of Norris and Dreiser, but they were still infrequent figures in the fictions aimed as Yezierska's were at a popular market.

Plot. The attitude toward the heroine that results from these intentions is markedly different from her earlier writings. At least in the beginning of the book, Yezierska clearly planned to use her leading lady as a figure to be castigated and condemned. The novel begins with the interview by the ardent young heroine, Sonya Vronsky, a reporter for a Jewish newspaper, with John Manning, a cool, cultured representative from the new York aristocracy who has chosen to work among the new immigrants. Sonya sees Manning as a deliverer and a saint, and she is determined to get him as a husband. In order to impress Manning, Vronsky feels she needs better clothes, so she goes to the salon of a famous dress designer, Jacques Hollins, *né* Jaky Solomon, and persuades him to give her a gown. At their next meeting Sonya and Manning discuss the differences between them—Manning regrets his inability to be warm and spontaneous and feels "ashamed of his isolation from life" (61) while Sonya describes herself in detail:

I am a Russian Jewess, a flame, a longing. A soul consumed with hunger for heights beyond reach. I am the ache of unvoiced dreams, the clamor of suppressed desires. I am the unlived lives of generations stifled in Siberian prisons. I am the urge of ages for the free, the beautiful that never yet was on land and sea. (65)

When Manning plans to call on Sonya in her ghetto room she embarks on a total redecoration. The young girl again shows her daring resourcefulness by directly confronting the landlord, first by reminding him of the duty of a good Jew to help an orphan get a husband and finally by blackmailing him not only to repaint her room, but the hall and stairwell as well. In order to buy new furniture she is forced to go to a pawnbroker, who gives her the money she needs, but extracts a promise to pay him the $1,000 plus $500 if she gets married. Lured by these artifices, Manning invites Sonya to be his secretary at the settlement house. Out of their daily contact, Manning's love grows and on a drive to Manning's country estate, he proposes. After the wedding, however, Sonya realizes that "she had more to give than he needed—than he wanted" (174) and ensconced in his "solid, cold impersonal" (179) townhouse, Sonya finds that she is a "stranger to herself in this strange world" (179), confused by the elaborate table service at dinner, but even more by the restraint of her husband. She feels that "loneliness gathered over her, like the clutches of a cold hand" (182).

Into the troubled situation comes the pawnbroker, Honest Abe, who now demands his $1,500. Unable to pay, Sonya pawns her engagement ring. But guilt over her deceits destroys her ability to accept Manning's love. In a stormy scene he tries to overwhelm her, but her rejection of him leaves him feeling ashamed of his lust. The next morning he makes it clear that he is no longer interested in her. In turn, she tells him her true feelings about him and his settlement house—that both are lies and fakes. She reveals her debt to the pawnbroker and insists that she had lied to him for no purpose other than her own personal motives: "I'm no charity saint like you. I've done nothing for anybody. I lied—lied—lied! For me—me—myself" (235). But she justifies her action by claiming that she is better than he. Marrying her was part of his "Christian reform" whose only religion is "family pride" (236). He is a cold fish, "a man who talks high words about the soul and hasn't spirit enough to get even my body" (236–37).

Sonya sees the marriage now at an end and runs away. She goes back first to the newspaper office where she had once worked, but finds no sympathy from her friend Gittel, who calls her a Christian, or from the editor, Lipkin, a shy, intellectual man who had once loved her but now refuses to give her her old job back. Distraught, Sonya tries to get a job as a maid in a hotel, but is again rejected. Finally she finds a job as a waitress where she is revolted by the tough girls she works with, the fat, vulgar cook, the sight of chewing mouths, the coarse advances of the patrons. She overhears two men discuss the lack of good designers, however, and asks for and gets a job.

In her new career, Sonya finds "released passion of creation" (269) and her dress designs are an instant success. The popularity of her clothes brings to the factory her old acquaintance, Jacques Hollins, the designer, who now hires her to work with him. Intrigued by her unceasing joy of discovery in every stitch of her work, the interest he had had in her on their first meeting blossoms into real love. As Hollins explains to Sonya, he loves her because he knows everything about her and not, as she had tried with Manning, because she has pretended to be something she was not. After Sonya is divorced from Manning, she marries Hollins and opens a nonprofit dress shop on Grand Street so that the immigrant women will have access to beautiful things. In her last meeting with Manning, when he makes a passionate plea for her, she comforts him as a woman comforts a child and realizes that "at bottom we're all alike, Anglo Saxons or Jews, gentlemen or immigrants. . . . When we're hungry, we're hungry—even a gentleman when starved long enough can become a savage East Sider" (289). Aware finally of the difference between passion and love, she realizes that "It's we who die, but the spark of love, the flash of beauty from eye to eye, the throb from heart to heart goes on and on forever" (290).

Characterization.   In the creation of the characters, Yezierska showed a significant advance over her earlier short stories in the use of contrasts to emphasize the particular traits of her central figures. Played against Sonya is the figure of Gittel, who worked in the newspaper office with her, the thin, washed-out spinster, pining away over the unrequited love she feels for the poet-editor. Gittel has specifically rejected self-assertiveness, and even visits Sonya to tell her of Lipkin's suffering because Sonya has not responded to his love for her. For Gittel, failure has become a way of life. She says, "Failure is my religion. . . . I accept failure in love and in life. The deeper, the finer you are, the more you realize the vulgarity, the sordidness of success" (151). Gittel becomes the epitome of all those who love and lose and justify their failure by saying, "What else is there in life but failure if you're deep enough" (151). Yezierska contrasts Sonya, one who strove to achieve some heights in life but fell, with Gittel one who never tried and was left with the hollowness of existence. Gittel's rejection of the fallen Sonya shows the cruelty of self-rightousness that grows from such a starved existence. For Gittel, Sonya's maneuvers to get Manning are crazy dances intended to get the head of John the Baptist.

The three men provide interesting contrasts with one another. Lipkin, the editor of the Jewish newspaper, prefers, like Gittel, to watch in silence rather than actively pursue the love he desires. He is the dreamer, the poet who pours out emotions into his verse, who struggles daily against poverty, keeping his dull editing job because it permits him to use his mind, dreaming of a life of intellectual achievement. He is heartbroken, shabby, self-torturing in his persistent attention to the developing love of Manning for Sonya. The pitiful plea that Gittel makes on his behalf only emphasizes the pathos of the figure. His rejection of Sonya when she comes for help shows perhaps the narrow rigidity which comes from such a self-pitying attitude.

Lipkin's limitations point up the traits in Manning that originally attracted Sonya, the Anglo Saxon with his coolness, his cultivated voice and language, the casual elegance of his fine clothes. They are, of course, all surface features, but they have also become a shell, a suit of armor that has kept the emotional side of his nature from growing. Manning's concentration on the surface of things also limits his ability to perceive the ghetto world. To him, Sonya's artifices are the real ghetto world, and when he visits her room decorated expensively on borrowed money, he believes it to be the natural simplicity of the poor, exclaiming, "Why it's the glory of poverty that it enforces simplicity" (121). His ideas of helping the immigrants are also based on a lack of understanding. He believes that "friendly visitors" who tamper with basic cultural patterns and check up on charity recipients are a useful device, unaware that the ghetto residents resent their interference in time-honored customs. He is similarly blind in emotional matters. His response to his desire is a sense of shame, and his giving in to it is a "hurricane of emotion." Despite his talk about behaving in a less formal way, he is embarrassed by her overdemonstrativeness on the train and finds it necessary to resist her approaches as they unpack in their room after the wedding. At the reception given at his home for his new wife, he cannot understand her retreat to her room when she overhears herself ridiculed by his socialite friends. Instead he criticizes her failure to follow the social forms which control his existence.

If forms were the crucial focus of his life, marriage seems to have been a form that permitted him to express his emotions. When he feels extreme passion, all restraint disappears and he is almost animal-like in his lust, only to suffer extreme guilt at his display of feelings. His behavior at their breakup reveals the limit of his ability to comprehend his wife, and his settlement for them is coldly formal, accounting for neither his own feeling nor hers. His letter to her when she is struggling to survive as a waitress reveals his stolid self-righteousness. When Manning, after their long separation, meets Sonya, his passion again overcomes him and he tries to force himself on her, but for the first time he is able to see in himself the same primitive passion that he had rejected in her.

Between the two positions represented by Lipkin and Manning stands the figure of Hollins. Like Lipkin, he is an immigrant Jew filled with a desire for self-expression, but in his case that desire is funneled into a creative form that is both artistic and economically rewarding. His transformation from Jaky Solomon to Jacques Hollins has been the result of the drive for money and power, but he has not sacrificed the sensitivity he shares with Lipkin. Rather he has found a way of synthesizing the two elements through the medium of art. He says:

I'm a Jew—yes—but I'm more than a Jew, I'm an artist. An artist transcends his race. When I returned from Paris, I saw that my living must come from millionaires. And a Jaky Solomon, though he were a wizard of style, could not command the price of a Hollins. Heine, the poet, let himself be sprinkled with Christian convert drops and went through the tragic process of changing his religion, not because he was ashamed of his race, but because it left him free to give his art to the world unhindered by racial prejudices. (50)

The same control that marked Hollins's rise as a designer also marks his attitude toward love. His initial attraction to Sonya is never expressed, and although he watches her at her first luncheon with Manning, he makes no effort to pursue his interest. Only when they meet again at the dress factory does he reveal any emotion. Yet even then, he hires her for her artistic ability. His love for her is based on a full knowledge of her faults as well as on his appreciation of her creativity. For him love is more than sudden passion: "It's on the ruins of our first blind romance, on the infatuation that breaks us that we come to understand the meaning of real love" (227).

In the creation of the character of Sonya, Yezierska's confusions about her purpose and conflicts about her message are further confounded by her changing attitudes toward the heroine. She clearly wants to show how Sonya's distorted ambition produced her self-centered actions, but she is also concerned with pointing up the failings of both the Jewish and Gentile worlds. She seems much more aware of the literary currents of her day and attempts to incorporate ideas garnered from the naturalist movement with Deweyesque theories of education and evolution, while at the same time preserving her sense of Old World values and the importance of self-reliance. Her heroine was, by turns, repulsive, attractive, vicious, and generous. Only Yezierska's skill in endowing her with vitality and strength redeems her. Sonya, rejecting passivity as a woman's role, is willing to go after the things she wants with incredible aggressiveness. Her immediate attraction to Manning seems based less on love than on sheer greed for the life he represents to her. Her aim is to end her poverty; she would be a philanthropist, she tells herself, but first she must end her poverty. She is, as Gittel says, "crazy for power" (15). But the ardor, the vitality, the vibrancy with which she carries out her maneuvers endow the figure with a certain charm. Her deliberate cunning in trapping the landlord into thinking she was a "chorus girl" (prostitute) and then blackmailing him into fixing up her room is coldblooded. A total egoist, she talks to herself in the mirror, admires her own power. She expresses more than just human greed, for the force which drives her is larger than mere human pettiness. "She was a planet on fire, rushing toward a darker star with which she must merge to complete their double destiny" (109). The fact that Yezierska is aware of Sonya's delusions is made apparent by the subsequent events in the novel. The suspicion that she was not achieving the beauty she searched for in her cold-blooded pursuit of Manning becomes all too apparent after the marriage. She realizes that the magnificent townhouse in which they live has become a prison; the servants, jailers; and the beautiful possessions, mere superficialities. The beauty she finds in marrying Manning is not the real beauty she has been seeking. Only after she runs away does she begin to understand what it is she really is seeking. As she discovers the joy of creativity, she learns the source of true fulfillment in life. In marrying Hollins she finds the synthesis that counts—the merger of the individual fulfillment with the unity of two people. Only then can she understand that without that kind of unity, humanity is trapped "by the brute passion which lies like a sleeping dog within the consciousness of the divine soul" (291).

  Literary Influences.   Such an attitude toward human relations indicates that Yezierska was aware of some of the new theories of psychology and philosophy current at the time. Whether these new influences were acquired from her association with Dewey or from her reading, they represent a new approach to her writing. The use of the Salome legend, with its strong feminist bias, a substantial leaning on the Emersonian doctrine of self-reliance, a development of a theory of the artist's role in society, and literary naturalism provide the substructure on which the novel depends, giving it not only a broader significance, but also causing a great deal of confusion.

  The Salome legend permitted Yezierska to add a mythic dimension to her heroine, connecting her with all women who dared challenge conventional feminine restraint in order to capture the men they love. Viewed this way, Sonya Vronsky becomes an individual of peculiar power, imaginatively and resourcefully combating all the elements in her environment which would keep her from finding the success she pursued with such single-minded fervor. Instead of being crushed by her poverty and the limitations of her immigrant background, she defies them. Like the legendary dancer, Sonya's victory is a hollow one that not only fails to bring the love she expects, but plunges her into even deeper misery than she had known before. Unlike Salome, however, Sonya learns from her experience and is able to find a way of reconciling herself to life.

Such a "superwoman" meshes somewhat loosely with the Emersonian doctrine of self-reliance. Sonya's nonconformity, her refusal to be bound by the limitations of her traditions, her determination to follow the dictates of her own will—all these traits find support in Emerson's essay. In addition, the treatment of Hollins's and Sonya's dress-designing careers as art is also supported by Emerson's belief that all examples of human creativity are equally valuable, and that the distinction between the utilitarian and the artistic is false.

By making Sonya a figure of the artist, Yezierska was also relying on the romantic tradition, of which Emerson was a part, of the special role and special freedoms that the artist is entitled to in society. Since artists in their search for beauty enrich all people by connecting them with higher spiritual values, they have not only a right, but even a necessity, to step beyond ordinary bounds. Because they dare to reach higher, artists may gain new insights that lead to better understanding of the human condition, but they also may plunge to greater depths and into greater errors. Sonya's view of herself as representing all the mute generations behind her lifts her out of the multitude of immigrant women, and since artists in their search for the beautiful may also follow false leads which bring them greater suffering than ordinary mortals, Sonya's failure plunges her into far greater depths than is suffered by the other characters in the novel. Yezierska apparently felt it necessary to tie this artistic vision to the ordinary needs of ordinary people, to make her heroine also just another immigrant girl. To satisfy this goal, to provide a happy ending for her novel, she has the figure of Hollins conveniently appear. All the fairy-tale elements of the Cinderella story which she seems to have rejected at the beginning are suddenly revived. The silent lover of the opening chapters miraculously appears, captures the heroine, and they live happily ever after. The only remnant of the artistic dream that remains is the fact that Sonya continues to work after her marriage.

The most important influence in the novel, however, is literary naturalism.[19] Lipkin's conversation with Sonya on life as a constant struggle between the weak and the powerful reflects the Social Darwinism of Norris, Dreiser, and Crane and the concluding words of the novel, describing humanity as caught by passions and forces it cannot control, follows the psychological determinisms of the naturalist tradition. Sonya's all-consuming egoism is reminiscent of Sister Carrie, and the seduction of Manning is as inevitable as that of Hurstwood. The definition of the characters in terms of their inescapable heredity— Manning the cold Anglo Saxon and Sonya the passionate Oriental— further extends the determinism inherent in the naturalist position. Like other heroes and heroines of naturalism who lead essentially amoral lives, Sonya is basically repellent, but redeemed by the sheer energy, vitality, life-force that she represents. Unfortunately, literary naturalism created its own philosophic dilemma that Yezierska was as incapable of solving as were the other followers of the tradition. If all society is controlled by outside forces, if no man is capable of moving beyond the limitations imposed by his heredity and surroundings, how do these leading characters defy those forces? How is it that Sonya Vronsky can overcome her past while the rest of her society fails? Although the authors do create such characters, the motivation remains unexplained. This strain of naturalism is a significant factor in the novel, yet Yezierska here, too, pulled away from the logical conclusions of the tradition. By permitting Sonya to learn from her experience, she had modified the inexorable path of naturalism. This faith in education is perhaps Dewey's influence, for it was a basic element of his philosophy that education can and does influence human behavior, modifying man's basic egocentricism for socially desirable aims.

The Jewish Tradition. With all these influences at work, it is not surprising that the Jewish tradition is submerged. In some cases it even seems distorted. The pawnbroker and the landlord are stereotyped figures who represent the worst features of the ghetto. Hollins has no remorse at rejecting his Jewish name and background, and Sonya herself shows little awareness of the beliefs of her people and has no hesitancy about marrying a Gentile. Yet Yezierska did preserve aspects of her heritage that finally dominate the novel. Sonya's rejection of her early materialistic attitude is tied directly to the Jewish emphasis on spiritual values. There is an assumption of the value of the community spirit of the Jewish world; when Sonya flees her Christian husband, it is to return to her Jewish past. The failure of the mixed marriage may be seen as a condemnation of that practice. Sonya's friends from the ghetto contrast favorably with Manning's, for they emerge as warm and generous people. The numerous Biblical references attest to Yezierska's own dependence on her heritage. Only in asserting a woman's right to control her own life does Yezierska break directly with traditions; yet, by ending her book with Sonya's marriage, Yezierska was endorsing a primary command of her faith.

This ending, however, clashes discordantly with the clearly feminist message of the novel. That Yezierska was only tangentially concerned with women's rights is evident from her rejection of the overt actions in that area of her model, Rose Pastor Stokes. Yet Sonya Vronsky is so strong a figure that she could not help but exemplify the right of a woman to determine her own life. There is no question that Sonya will work at her own career even after her marriage to Hollins and that her fulfillment as a person depends on it. The contrast between her life with Hollins and her life with Manning is a direct condemnation of the inactivity of the typical rich wife. Although Yezierska seemed to feel marriage was a necessity for Sonya, it is marriage that permits freedom of expression that she is supporting here.

Critical Reception.   The reviews of the novel were only partially favorable. While the figure of Sonya attracted the most attention, she was alternately condemned for her "depravity of spirit" or praised for her vitality.[20] The explicitness of the love story bothered one critic and another condemned the "orgy of emotions."[21] One reviewer recognized Yezierska's more serious intentions to show "how men and women helplessly and unknowingly destroy themselves and each other in the blind uprising of brute passions."[22] Most often, though, the reviews focused on the surface features of the ghetto world and Yezierska's ability to sketch that world was praised.

Attempting to join all these different strands would tax the resources of the most skilled writer. Yezierska at this point in her career was just beginning to perfect her technique as a writer, and her handling of so many disparate philosophic strands was bound to be disappointing. The lack of time for more careful writing, the confusions in her personal

life as she attempted to cope with her Hollywood experiences, prevented her from writing a better book. The book was, however, not
only published, but also sold as a magazine serial and made into a
movie.

Children of Loneliness

The stories which were included in the collection *Children of Loneliness* exhibit the same erratic quality as *Salome*. Occasional tales flash
with the intensity of her earlier works, but for the most part the fictions
here show the signs of hasty construction and partial thinking. Many of
the themes and situations are similar to those she had explored in
Hungry Hearts and others introduce ideas that would be more fully
treated in later novels. Once more, the total work is most valuable for
its explorations of the character of the Jewish immigrant woman,
caught between the two worlds of her Old World past and the new
American one, who struggles to define herself and find the right path
between conflicting pulls.

The Immigrant Woman and Her Isolation.   The title story is
one of the most effective treatments of this theme. In it, the young
woman, Rachel, has graduated from college and returned to her home
on the Lower East Side. Feeling herself to be fully Americanized, she is
appalled by her parents' Old World habits, symbolized by their lack of
table manners. She spends her first week home criticizing them to such
an extent that her father finally explodes:

You think you can put our necks in a chain and learn us new tricks? You think
you can make us over for Americans? We got through till fifty years for our
lives eating in our own old way—(102)

For the old man, a scholar who has continued to devote his life to the
study of the sacred texts, his daughter's attitude "smacked of apostasy,
anti-Semitism and the aping of the Gentiles" (103). Rachel, on the
other hand, can only cringe at the thought of how ignorant, dirty, and
low her parents would appear to her new college friends, especially
Frank Baker, the young man she has met at school. As the argument
continues, father and daughter shouting vituperations at each other,
the young girl gathers up her possessions and leaves her parents' home.

When she has settled in her own spotlessly clean room, however, she finds that she has chosen a "loneliness that's death" (110). Once more she returns to visit her old home where her emotions seesaw wildly. At first, hearing her father chant the ancient prayers, she is overwhelmed with love for this "mystic spirit stranger who could thrill with such impassioned rapture" (112). But at the sight of the dirt and confusion of the home, her sense of love dissolves, only to be replaced with pity at the sight of the "wrung-dry weariness" (116) of their faces. Torn by the conflict that rages within her, she leaves, feeling as if she had "torn away from the flesh and blood of her own body" (116).

At her meeting with Frank, she romanticizes the prospect of their love. Frank has come to New York to work in an East Side settlement and is enraptured by what he considers "the poetry which the immigrant is daily living" (119).Their conversation reveals the chasm between their views. For Frank, these people have "a beautiful home life, the poetic devotion between parents and children . . ." (119) while Rachel describes it as "the battle to the knife . . ." (119). The final break comes when Frank refers to the ghetto people as "social types" (120). Realizing that she is only an interesting specimen to him, Rachel ends their date abruptly. At the end of the story she sits alone with her dilemma still unsolved. "I can't live with the old world, and I'm yet too green for the new. I don't belong to those who gave me birth or to those with whom I was educated" (122). Yet her courage returns with the dawn and although her future still seems bleak to her, she is aware that she is not alone: "I'm one of the millions of immigrant children, children of loneliness, wandering between worlds that are at once too old and too new to live in" (123).

In this story Yezierska has stated the case for the parents' generation more strongly than in earlier treatments. The fight between the father and daughter deals with superficial matters, but masks far deeper concerns, resentments and guilt. Given the all-encompassing nature of Jewish ritual in every-day life the daughter's behavior seems to the father a falling away for the old, God-given precepts and in his anger his character is suffused with the power of an Old Testament prophet:

Pfui on the morals of America. No respect for old age. No fear for God. Stepping with your feet on all the laws of the holy Torah. A fire should burn out the whole new generation. They should sink into the earth, like Korah. (103)

The old prayers are a source of comfort and joy. As the father chants, he loses all his anger and condemnation; he has found a "shelter from the storms of life that the artist finds in his art . . . (104). The mother, too, is portrayed in a loving fashion. Her joy at having her daughter home is expressed in the care with which she prepares her meals: "How I was hurrying to run by the butcher before everybody else, so as to pick out the grandest, fattest piece of *brust!* . . . . And I put my hand away from my heart and put a whole fresh egg into the *lotkes*" (107). Her devotion to her husband is also captured as she is pictured "with a self-effacing stoop of humility" (114) urging him to eat his dinner.

Rachel, on the other hand, is less powerful as a protagonist, but the honesty with which her confusions and guilt are conveyed make her a striking figure. By exaggerating the girl's cruel treatment of her parents, Yezierska has emphasized the second generation's inability to separate that which is valuable from the superficial elements in their background. She can see only complete acceptance or total rejection of her past. In her first blaze of anger, she sees them as "ugly and gross and stupid" (106) while she regards herself as "all sensitive nerves" (106). To stay with them would mean descending to their level and a loss of all her newfound values. Yet her rejection of them brings guilt and self-pity. She is both drawn back to them and repulsed by their ways. The only resolution Yezierska permits her heroine is the realization that to outsiders like Frank, they are merely interesting specimens of sociology. By rejecting her college boyfriend, Rachel is implicitly acknowledging her identification with her own people, her awareness that she must continue to live in the no-man's-land between two cultures. Rachel here has become a figure through whom Yezierska could serve as spokeswoman for those who had not yet felt themselves as members of the American world, but who could no longer feel a part of the Jewish world from which they came.

Several of the stories describe the problems faced by those who were thus isolated. In one, "A Bed for the Night," the problems are the material ones of needing food, clothing, and shelter. In this tale, the narrator has just been released from a hospital to find that her ghetto room has been rented to another person. Despite the horrors of rooming-house life, she can find no adequate substitute. She visits a wealthy patron, "a childless woman with a house full of rooms to herself" (166), but receives no help. A visit to the "Better Housing Bureau" only produces forms to fill out and an inquisition. A rich sister tells her she looks shabby, but does not offer to pay for a room for her. Her boss at work only makes provocative suggestions, and the sight of a beggar in the park chills her. In the end, one old woman takes her into her poor home only to shove her out in the morning.

Choosing Values. More often the stories deal with the problems of choosing values. In "Dreams and Dollars," the choice to the narrator lies between materialism and ideals. The narrator, a young girl, has gone to visit her married sister in Los Angeles and is horrified by the spiritual emptiness of her life, the gaudy furniture, the card-playing, the flashy cars. While she is able to appreciate the affectionate nature and generous instincts of these people, it is only when she goes back to her old friend who is a ghetto poet does she begin to understand why these people have chosen as they have:

"Don't you see, little heart," he says to her. . . . "The dollars are their dreams. They eat the fleshpots with the same passionate intensity that they once fasted in faith on the Day of Atonement. Let them eat. They have been hungry for so many centuries. Give them a chance for a few generations. They'll find their souls again." (202)

The spirit of generosity with which Yezierska concluded this tale is replaced by condemnation in "Brothers." In this tale, Moisha, a young immigrant man, works, saves, and finally borrows enough money to bring his family to this country to escape the pogroms of Russia. Instead of being satisfied, his brothers complain of the dark ghetto rooms. While Moisha continues to work to support the family, his brothers go to school, one to become a dentist, the other a poet, but neither contributes anything to the support of the family. At the end of the story the dentist, now successful and rich, is spied dressed for his wedding, to which he has not invited his own poor relations.

The Artist and the Need for Community. In two of the stories Yezierska takes up the problem of the artist, both of which stress the need to keep one's ties to one's community. In "The Song Triumphant" a poet who has enjoyed great success as a writer of popular songs abandons his career and returns to his ghetto world when he realizes that he has sold himself for the emptiness of material success. Only when he has taken a job in a factory does he begin to find once again the spiritual beauty that had eluded him. In "To the Stars," another artist, this time a young woman writer, finds her inspiration in the life of the people around her. Rebuffed in her efforts to learn formal writing techniques at college, she has decided to use her immigrant English and wins a short-story contest. The story is crowded with many incidents, far too many for a fiction of this length. In it Yezierska has tried to cover the young woman's efforts to get into college, her meeting with a helpful college president, her difficulties as a cook in a restaurant, the life in a rooming house run by an excitable Jewish woman, her hunger and illness, as well as her final success. Much of this material would eventually find its way into her later novels, and part of it had already appeared in the earlier "My Own People." The story's episodic quality indicates that far more work would be needed before it could be considered fully developed.

Yet, if Yezierska was anxious to show the value of remaining true to one's heritage, she also questioned how valid such a position could be in the New York ghetto as she knew it. In "The Lord Giveth" she created the character of an old rabbi who had once been a famous scholar in Russia. The values of the New York ghetto are contrasted against both the Old World community and the American world. In this tale an old Hebrew scholar longs for the respect and support he had received in Europe. He remembers that in Russia he had "people coming to him from far and near to learn wisdom from his lips" (209–10). Instead of such honor, he experiences in New York the indifference of his Americanized Jewish neighbors. Yet, when the family is dispossessed, these same neighbors rally round the family, find them a new home, and raise money to buy food. As they are enjoying a feast purchased from this generosity, however, there appears a representative of the charity which has been giving them funds. Seeing the expensive food, she accuses them of lying about their poverty and cancels their allowance. Thus, the ghetto world, while not as caring as the European community, is painted as being at least more humane than the Americans with their system of scientific charity.

Narrative Essays. Perhaps the best work in the book are the narrative essays in which she reviews the immigrant's illusions about America, the inevitable discouragement and then the final battle for a more mature understanding. In "America and I" the focus is on the immigrant's dream of finding work that expressed her creativity, that here "the unlived lives of generations clamoring for expression" (35) would through her have an outlet. The narrator recounts her working experience—the first, while still a young child, as a servant in an Americanized family. Her dream here is simply to earn money with which to buy herself American clothes, but the family feels that the room and board they provide and the opportunity to live with them is sufficient compensation. Heartbroken, crushed because she had trusted the Americans to provide the money to replace her immigrant rags, she leaves. Her next job is in a sweatshop in a basement sewing on buttons. Working from the dark of morning to the dark of night, she earns barely enough for food and rent for her bed "a mattress on the floor in a rat-hole of a room occupied by a dozen other immigrants" (41). Only the fact that she has her evenings free compensates for the barrenness of her life. But when the busy season starts even that is taken away, and because she complains, she is fired. As a trained factory worker her life becomes easier, but the creative expression still eludes her. Her efforts to break out of the mold are met with indifference or misunderstanding. The English teacher in the factory thinks learning the language would solve her problem; the vocational-guidance worker talks of efficiency and the happy worker, but advises her to stay with her present job. The America of her dreams, the America that would offer her the opportunity for self-expression, she realizes, is only an illusion. In her attempt to find the real America, she begins to read American history and learns of the difficulties endured by the Pilgrims. From this knowledge comes the understanding that the America she is seeking—the America which is the idea—is still in the making. By writing stories about life in the ghetto, she feels she is contributing to the making of that idea. The theme of the essay is one that had appeared frequently in previous writings, the difference here being the focus on work. The incidents she tells to illustrate it are powerful, so powerful that they assume more significance than the essay. The parts are more than the whole and provide a moving glimpse into the life of the domestic servant and the sweatshop worker.

Two of the narrative essays grow out of experiences which had happened to her after she had become a writer. In "An Immigrant Among the Editors" she is apparently drawing on her meeting with Frank Crane, during which she had persuaded him to review *Hungry Hearts*. In the fictional piece, she has revised the event so that the narrator, a young woman who writes in the garbled tongue of her immigrant group, seeks out different editors of American magazines in an attempt to find a publisher of her stories. The first, with the "terrible clean face and cold eyes of this clean, cold higher-up" (59), runs out of his office to escape her. The second demands logic and reason rather than the emotionalism of her tales. The third gives her a psychological study of madness to read. These three men she views as reformers, "holy social workers" (66) rather than human beings with compassionate understanding. A fourth editor, however, does have the understanding to appreciate her work and he buys her story for $200. Later when she has achieved success, she finds that other budding writers come to her for help. At first she turns them down, but shocked by her own brutality she reviews her actions and becomes aware of how she too has lost the "friendly understanding of humanity" (68). The paradox which she is pointing to is that all yearn for success, and are angered by those who fail to help them, but when they themselves reach their goals they, too, become hard. Only through force of effort can one's sense of humanity be maintained.

In "You Can't Be an Immigrant Twice" Yezierska describes a recent experience in traveling in steerage, repeating her first journey to the United States. She traveled in this fashion because although she is now financially secure, she feels guilty about enjoying the comforts her money could buy while others still suffered. Also she sees it as an opportunity to "feel with" those new immigrants in the hardships they have to suffer. She is aware that conditions have improved from the time she and her family first embarked, but she is humiliated by the treatment the third-class passengers must endure in submitting to a physical examination. At the first meal on board she is shocked by the service—"Plates thrown at you. Thick plates . . . bread cut so thick that it took your hunger away" (264–65)—and by the table manners of the people. She realizes that years of success have spoiled her, that she no longer can eat the coarse bread and thick pieces of meat. Transferring to second-class quarters, she continues to visit with the steerage passengers, for she finds that the most interesting people are there. She is captivated by the Czechoslovakian peasant women, whose faces reflected "the majesty and stillness of the open fields they came from" (267). Yet she was aware of the racial conflict that existed between the various national groups. The vitality of the people, their open expressions, their unbridled feelings compensate for their lack of understanding. Their faith and hope in America, their sense of adventure gave to even "the oldest of them . . . the glow of young people in love with life" (268). The dangers of the American materialism are tentatively suggested in the incident in which she takes a young painter to show him the first-class quarters, which leads him to say, "I'll give up painting and get money somehow easier, if money can make all this difference" (269).

The form of the essay is an interview with a reporter over three-quarters of which are quotations by Yezierska. The opening section includes a brief résumé of her early life, as vaguely told as were the Hollywood press releases, and the lack of form in the essay can be attributed to the informal nature of the interview. It is probable that Yezierska was seeking to use this material to create a story, but as it stands, it is only a fleeting suggestion of what she might have done with it. There are among her papers no manuscripts on this theme, and none of her later fiction deals with it. Perhaps if she had had more leisure or felt more at ease with herself and her position she might have been able to transmute it into a moving story, but in its present state it seems to have been included simply to fill out the published volume.

Perhaps the best-integrated work in the volume is "Mostly About Myself." Despite its title it seems to be no more about herself than any of her other narratives. Here, as she had in *Hungry Hearts,* her concept of the "self" had less to do with the outward events but depended entirely on the interior sense of being—that self which dreamed, was disillusioned, yet fought its way back to dreams. Although incidents which may be autobiographical are included, the thrust of the piece is the spiritual and emotional journey of the immigrant seeking a new and better life. The focus is less on the work experience as it was in "America and I," but both pieces are concerned with the need for expression and communication. In the opening lines, the narrator speaks of the centuries in Russia in which "my people had no voice" (9). Describing the family, she presents a very moving portrait of the mother who "dried out her days fighting at the pushcarts for another potato, another onion into her bag" (9). The effect on the narrator's childhood is baleful. "Life had crushed my mother so without knowing it she fed defeat with the milk of her bosom into the blood and bones of her children" (20). When the child wants to have a birthday party like her friend Becky, the pawnbroker's child, the mother's angry response is "Wouldn't it be better if you was never born already. . . . You ought to light a black candle on your birthday. You ought to lie on your face and curse the day you were born" (22).

Determined to escape the deprivations that clouded the mother's life, the young girl rails at the only work available to her and takes to writing as an antidote to the terrible loneliness she feels. Despite the joy of her first success, she is also aware of her failure to capture perfectly the image she had tried to convey. Drawing on Whitman, whom she quotes, she found that the failure of her writings to measure up to her expectations spurs her on to further creative work. Thus her disadvantages have become a kind of advantage. So, too, her years of poverty have given her firsthand knowledge that other authors lack. Instead of staying simply as the angry rebel of her first writings, she has become both one who demands that America perform as its immigrant population dreamed it would, and an affirmer of America whose very flaws vitalize those it does not kill.

The essay is valuable in showing the new reconciliation that Yezierska had achieved between her past and her present by visualizing herself both as "the mad mob at a mass meeting clapping with their hands and stamping with their feet to their leader: 'Speech! Speech!'" and "the bewildered leader struggling to say something and make myself heard through the deafening noise" (10). She also presents a suggestion of a definition of her own writings not as literature, which she considered "decoration," but as "real." But that reality, she feels, is closer to the spiritual quality that transcends the merely superficial, suggesting a strong mystic strain in her nature. The tone of the essay is strongly affirmative, but it is also clear that the sense of her role and of her path is still confused. The anecdotes sprinkled through the essay are still the most valuable to the reader.

Critical Reception. The critical reception was less enthusiastic than that given *Hungry Hearts*. But among Jewish critics the issue of her language was a matter of dispute.[23] The feeling was that by using the broken English of the immigrant, she was mocking her people. Dialect, up to that time, had been the material of the comedian, most notably Montagu Glass, whose characters had made frequent appearances in popular magazines. But while Glass was indeed caricaturing Yiddish speakers, Yezierska was attempting to cope with a different problem. On the one hand, she was interested in suggesting the difference of speech, and thereby indicating the isolation of the immigrants from the mainstream of Americans. She was, in addition, concerned with maintaining the vigor and bite of Yiddish whose power would be lost in more correct translation. Furthermore, it would distort the personality of her characters to pretend that they spoke proper English. If she had translated their dialogues which normally would have been spoken in Yiddish into proper English, these necessary artistic values would be lost. In her writings Yezierska had taken a step forward in realism by using the immigrant speech for her characters; later a more skillful writer, Henry Roth, would in *Call It Sleep* find a better method, using correct English and poetic translations for the Yiddish speakers and reserving broken English for those times his characters actually spoke in English. But Yezierska's accomplishment should not be minimized simply because it was not a perfect solution.

The effects of Yezierska's separation from the ghetto world and of her life as a Hollywood celebrity can be seen in the two books that grew out of that experience. Uncomfortable with her newfound wealth, she cries out at the dangers of materialism; guilty over her neglect of her people, she romanticizes some aspects of the ghetto world. But at the same time, these two books also show increased intellectual development and flashes of potential power. The ghetto world, painted as vividly as ever in a few swift strokes, has a deeper, richer texture as a few characters emerge in more full detail, and her appreciation of its values shows an increased depth of understanding. In her portraits of women, particularly the young immigrant girl, she has broadened her perspective to include the problems of the Americanized daughter, and the difficulties of success. Many of these elements would come together in her next work, which would be the most significant achievement of her early years.

Chapter Four
Breadgivers

By 1924, Yezierska seems to have found a measure of peace. After a trip to Europe, she lived for a while at the Grosvenor Hotel on lower Fifth Avenue and then in an apartment on Waverly Place—a choice that was psychologically suitable—near enough to the scenes of her adolescence that provided the core of her writing, yet fashionable enough to be part of the "uptown" world. In addition, she was close to the intellectual life centered in Greenwich Village although there is no evidence that she was part of any movement there. She had established friendships with some of the New York literary community, such as William Lyons Phelps, Frank Crane, Glen Frank, Fannie Hurst, and Dorothy Canfield Fisher. Dining with them at the Algonquin, the famed center for the literati, she could at least gossip about writing and feel herself an accepted American author. The money earned from the movies of *Hungry Hearts* and *Salome* was enough to support her, thus dismissing from her mind the spectre of poverty that so haunted her. And her writing reflected the relative calm, the opportunity to revise and rethink, so that many of the themes from her earlier work came together with fresh vigor and greater maturity. The novel *Breadgivers,* written during this period, is undoubtedly her finest work during these early years.

Here, more thoroughly than she would ever do again, she explored the many aspects of the Jewish woman's experience in America, offering a variety of portraits detailing the blighted hopes, the weary, unending struggle against poverty and filth or the hollowness of wealth without spiritual values, but most of all the unresolvable tensions between the ancient Jewish mores that assumed male domination and the American ideal of individual freedom. The subtitle, *A Struggle Between a Father of the Old World and a Daughter of the New,* indicates the main focus on the psychological tensions between the obstinate patriarch and his equally stubborn daughter, of love distorted by pride and poverty, of the pain of inescapable guilt. The conflicting tensions that had marked both her life and her work found here a successful expression—the wish to become part of America versus the pull of tradition and family; a woman's desire for self-fulfillment versus the wish for home, husband and children; the desire for material comforts versus the demands for intellectual achievement. She was able finally to direct her wish to be a spokeswoman into productive channels.

Plot

The story concerns the coming to maturity of Sara, one of the four daughters of Reb Smolinsky, and traces her rise from the eleven-year-old herring peddler, pinched and starving, fighting to earn the few pennies that would put food on the family table, to her final achievement as a teacher with a college degree, married to a man who shared her heritage and her goals. The story is told by Sara and reflects her early childish illusions as well as her adult vision. Yet Sara's story is inseparable from the life of the family and the ghetto world in which they live. The family's struggle is not only against the sordidness of poverty, but also against the oppressive tyranny of the father who invokes his right as a man and a scholar to dominate the women who surround him. Their miserable tenement apartment is crowded by his books "on the shelf, on the table, on the window sill and in the soap boxes line up against the wall."[1] Having chosen to maintain the Old World Hebraic tradition of devotion to prayer and study, he fully expects others to support and honor him without question and considers himself as the religious and ethical leader of the community. He alternately bullies and preaches at his wife and four daughters with blind self-righteousness. Although the family teeters precariously on the edge of poverty, he makes no attempt to earn money; instead he expects the best portion of food at the table, the best room in the home for his study, an unruffled atmosphere, and even the right to make extravagant donations to charity. They are his due, for he regards himself as the light for others in the community and by his piety insuring for his wife the place in Heaven which she, as a woman, could not achieve on her own.

The mother accepts her status unquestioningly, melts at the least sign of her husband's pleasure, and is inspired by his holiness. But although she is shrewd and hardworking, the struggle to maintain the family wears on her frayed nerves, and she alternately nags at her husband and screams curses at her daughters, each of whom responds in a unique way. Bessie, the oldest, is the burden bearer. She works all day at the factory, brings bundles home to earn extra money, helps her mother with the housework and gives every cent of her wages to her father. Mashah, whose love of beauty had turned inward upon herself, lives "for the pleasure she got from her beautiful face" (4), and is unperturbed by the dirt and trouble surrounding her. Instead, she spends her money buying trifles to accentuate her appearance and spends her time at concerts in the park. Fania is the intellectual of the group, and although she too works to support the family, she finds a measure of escape in night school classes and in the books she gets from the local library. But the focus of the novel is Sara, the youngest. She shares some of the traits of each of her sisters, but is distinguished by her courage, defiance and energy. Called "Blut and Eisen"—Blood and Iron,—she refuses to accept the impotence imposed by age and sex; when all her sisters are out of work, the rent unpaid, and her father jailed for striking the landlady, it is she who takes the last money the family had to buy herring which she successfully peddles in the street.

Their situation is eased when the mother persuades the father to give up his room so that she can take in boarders, and the older girls find work. But a new tension develops in the family as the daughters, despite their lack of dowry, find suitors. Instead of rejoicing, the father sees their potential marriages as threatening his source of income. Bessie's friend is a cutter in a factory who hopes to open his own shop and sees in Bessie "a person who knows how to save a dollar and cook a good meal and help me yet in the shop" (45). His interest in Bessie is based less on love than convenience, but he is shocked to discover that her father holds a similar view. "Don't forget when she gets married, who'll carry me the burden from this house? She earns me the biggest wage . . ." (45). Berel, who had abandoned his own religious scruples, considers the father a beggar and refuses to pay him for the privilege of marrying Bessie. Instead, he simply marries the next available woman. Despite Bessie's anguish, the father complacently denies any responsibility for his daughter's suffering.

Mashah's suitor, Jacob Novak, easily satisfies the father's economic criteria, for he is the son of a wealthy department store owner, but is rejected for his impiety. A pianist who has rented an apartment in the ghetto in order to practice for his debut, Jacob has attracted Mashah by the beauty of his music and has been drawn to her in turn by the warmth and passion of her response. While Reb Smolinsky objects to the fact that Jacob violates the Sabbath by his practicing, the romance actually is broken by Jacob's father whose very appearance "hollered money, like a hundred cash registers ringing up dollars" (58) and who objects to such a poverty-stricken girl as a daughter-in-law. Although Jacob tries to reestablish the relationship, the father forbids it, and Mashah, like Bessie, succumbs to Reb Smolinsky's rules.

Fania and her poet, Morris Lipsky, fare no better. Their romance is discovered by Reb Smolinsky when he cavalierly opens his daughter's mail. The father, goaded by his wife's accusation that he is destroying his daughters' chances for marriage, decides to find suitable husbands himself, and when Morris comes to ask permission to marry Fania, he finds the father entertaining another potential suitor and is treated as if he did not even exist. The father taunts Fania for her suitor's poverty and forces her to abandon her young man.

Reb Smolinsky's years of prayer and study have ill-prepared him for worldly affairs, but he now takes over the family management, totally oblivious to his shortcomings. He marries Mashah off to a supposed diamond dealer who turns out to be a charlatan, spending all his money on himself and barely giving his wife enough to maintain the home and feed the children. Bessie is literally sold to Zalman, a fifty-six-year-old, widowed fish peddler with six unruly children, and Fania is given to Abe Schumkler, a wealthy cloak-and-suit buyer from Los Angeles, who turns out to be a gambler. Each of the girls accepts the husband, for they see marriage as the only escape from the father's tyranny and are totally obedient to their father's commands. Then the father uses the money he received from the fish peddler to buy a grocery business in a small New Jersey town, only to be swindled out of his last penny. The mother's herculean efforts save the family from total disaster, but Sara, who serves as the store's saleslady, finds life away from the crowded ghetto lonely and bleak. When her father rails at her for trusting a customer for two cents, she storms out, determined to make her own way in the world. In her last argument with her father, she denies his right under Jewish law to control her life, and declares, "I'm going to live my own life. Nobody can stop me. I'm not from the old country. I'm American!" (138).

Difficult as Sara's declaration of independence was to state, it was even more difficult to achieve, and the second section of the novel details the painful struggle of the seventeen-year-old girl to carve out her own future. As single-minded as the father in his piety, Sara concentrates on her dream of becoming a schoolteacher. She returns to New York, enrolls in night school and supports herself as an ironer in a laundry. She forces herself to ignore the filth of her dingy room, the jarring clatter of the tenement, but the thirty-four cents a day she allots herself for food leaves her constantly hungry and the bitter cold saps her energy. Her despair at her way of life is accentuated by her terrible loneliness, and the real temptation to abandon her struggle comes from her need for companionship. Yet she resists, refusing to visit her parents, rejecting her sisters' suggestions that she marry. Even when her devoted mother begs her to visit, she can only say: "I'd do anything for you. I'd give you away my life. But . . . every little minute must go to my studies . . . I could see you later. But I can't go to college later" (171). The prospect of love, however, provides the biggest stumbling block. Max Goldstein, a friend of Fania's from Los Angeles, is charmed by the independence and lack of coquetry of the young woman, as she is by his energy and joyous grasp of life. The prospect of a comfortable, if dull, life with Max almost overwhelms her resolve. But, although she rejects his proposal, the knowledge that she has been loved and has loved in return provides her with new pride and assurance. A final disastrous visit with her father confirms her resolve to make her own way in the world.

Although Sara has succeeded in making her break with the Old World past, she has not yet found a way into the new. Her experiences at college accentuate the gulf between herself and the typical American college student. Unlike those well-groomed, carefree girls and boys, she has to work for her living and has only her Hester Street clothes. While they plan gay social outings, she slaves at the local laundry. She struggles with the required curriculum, unable to see its benefit, and revolts only over the required physical education course that is too much for her already overtaxed body. Although she is disappointed by the lack of interest of her overworked professors, she finds that her life experiences are illuminated by her studies in psychology, and if she is rebuffed by the younger instructors, she is accepted and helped by some of the older faculty. Her triumph comes at commencement when she is awarded the prize for the best essay and exults in the cheers of her fellow students. The final section of the book details Sara's journey back to her own people. With the money from the essay contest she is able to travel on a Pullman train, to buy new clothes in an uptown department store, to find a clean, quiet apartment. She glories now in her aloneness, "her precious privacy" (241). Nonetheless, she goes back to visit her family on Hester Street, only to discover that her mother is dying and that her father is in the clutches of a neighboring widow intent on marrying him for the insurance money. She is warmed by her sisters' affection, but as she listens to the wild sobbing that characterizes the mourning for her mother, she finds "her eyes dry and her heart numb" (255). Refusing to have her new dress cut, as Jewish mourning ritual demands, she feels a stranger among her own people.

Her sense of familial responsibility remains, however. Returning to look after her father, she finds that he has remarried barely thirty days after her mother's death, and that the new wife, having squandered all the death payment, now demands that the children support their father and herself. Coping with this new burden as best she can, Sara finds fulfillment in her work. True happiness comes with her growing friendship with Hugo Seelig, the principal of the school, an immigrant like herself who has succeeded not only in earning enough money, but who has retained his love of scholarship, a man who is Americanized yet respects the tradition from which he has sprung. Through him, Sara comes to see her father as he really is—a lonely old man, crushed by life but unable to understand it, with only his fanatic devotion to his tradition to sustain himself. With her new husband, Sara provides a home for her father. Sara has come full circle back to the place from which she started, but now living on a higher plane, enriched by knowledge and experiences of her life. In her now the Jewish tradition and the American are joined into a new amalgam that contains the best elements from each.

Characters

Mother and Daughters.   The characters in the novel are one of its strongest assets. As in her earlier works, Yezierska was able to create vivid types with a few swift sketches, and the characters are vibrantly alive. In addition, she was able here to show changes within her characters that did not jar against their original personalities. The mother with "faded eyes, her shape like a squashed barrel of yeast, and her face black and yellow with all the worries from the world" (30) is so revived by their improved economic condition that "She even began to laugh, once in a while" (29) and tell the children stories of happy times in her past, "drunk with the memories of old times" (31). Each of the sisters exists not only as they appear originally but as they are changed by their marriages—Fania who had given up the poor writer was now a "dressed-up, grand lady . . . (174):

Gone was the innocence of the young dreams from her eyes. Good eating, good sleeping and the sunshine of plenty breathed from her face. And she held her head high, as if she didn't come from the same family as the rest of us. But for all her shine, I could see in the shadowy places under her eyes thready lines of restlessness. (174–75)

Mashah, no longer the "young girl, standing proud in the power of her beauty" had repaired "the dingy darkness of her home with her love of beauty" (146):

With her own hands she had patched up the broken plaster on the wall and painted them a golden yellow. The rotten boards of the window sill and the shelves were hidden by white oilcloth and held in place by shining brass tacks . . . White curtains of the cheapest cheesecloth were on the one window, but hung with that grace that Mashah put into anything that she touched. (146)

But the beauty that was in the house had come out of Mashah's face.

The sunny colour of her pots and pans had taken the lustre out of her hair, and the soda with which she had scrubbed the floor so clean, and laundered her rags to white, had burned in and eaten the beauty out of her hands. (147)

The glow of love for her three children switches to sudden hate at the worrying fear of poverty. They have become the instrument that she says "chains me to this misery" (148).

The change in Bessie is the most severe. A burden-bearer even before she left her parents' home, her life is rougher as she manages her

husband's fish store. "Her thick arms . . . covered with the gummy
scales of the fish. Her face, her hair and her apron . . . thick with it"
(140). With her pitiful thick face "squeezed dry of hope or happiness"
(176), she bemoans the role of a stepmother:

> At first I sewed and scrubbed and killed myself cooking for Zalmon's
> children. But you can never do enough for them. . . . Nothing I do for these
> children is right for them. (177)

These blighted lives are crushingly real in and of themselves, but they
offer a sharp contrast to the Mother who suffered much as they did, but
who was sustained by a belief in the traditions she lived by and who, out
of love for her youngest daughter, travels through a bitter night's cold
to bring her a featherbed and looks at her with "sunken eyes gleaming
out of their black sockets with a dumb, pleading love" (170).

Even the suitors and husbands, given hardly more than a few lines,
are sharply rendered—Berel Bernstein, proud of the few dollars he has
saved, anxious to set up his own business who believes that in America
"everybody got to look out for themselves" (49); Jacob Novak, who had
about him "the sure richness of the higher up" (56), but who lacked the
courage to defy his father; shabby, long-haired Morris Lipkin who
writes fiery poems of love; Moe Mirsky, expansive in his false glitter,
"blowing his chest with pride and pleasure in himself" (149), cruelly
criticizing his work-worn wife. The portrait of Zalmon, the old fish
peddler, come to court Bessie stands out. He is no longer the man of
work:

> His black greasy beard spotted with scales from the fish . . . a big wart on
> his nose and his thick red lips . . . cracked open in the middle, who smelled
> of fish. (91)

He is instead transformed in the interests of romance:

> . . . the door opened and a smell of perfume filled our kitchen. A man
> entered. . . . He wore a new black suit and looked just like those wax figures
> in the show windows where they have clothes to hire for weddings . . . his
> hair barbered short and pasted down with vaseline and soaked in perfume.
> (99)

Even Sara's first suitor, Max Goldstein, who "clapped his hands and feet and shouted with laughter" at the cheap vaudeville show, is compelling in his honest acceptance of himself, full of "get rich quick schemes" and the warmth of his love.

The characters from the American world are less vivid, but they are far more rounded than in Yezierska's previous writings. The young psychology lecturer, Mr. Edman, while as stiff as earlier versions of similar characters, gains new life as Yezierska also shows him overworked and overdriven. And Hugo Seelig, the principal of the school, is a clear portrait of an Americanized Jew who has successfully combined the two influences. He helps the young teacher with gentleness as well as authority, is a dreamer not of the past but "a dreamer who had found his work among us of the East Side" (273). He conquers her father upon meeting him, by asking for Hebrew lessons and he sees in Sara's fight, not the hard heart she feared but "the fibre of a strong live spruce tree that grows in strength the more it's knocked about by the wind" (279).

The Father.   The strength of the novel rests upon the characterizations of the father Reb Smolinsky and his complex relationship with his daughters, especially Sara. At first the old man appears to be only a petty tyrant. He bullies his wife and children, lies without compunction to justify his actions, is self-righteous in using his religion. But however monstrous the father's actions sometimes seem, he is never simply a villain. He, like his daughters, is caught between two opposing ways of life. Clinging to the ideals of his heritage, he spends his days in prayer and study, realizing all the while that his role is no longer respected, driven by frustration to hit the irreverent landlady who desecrates his Holy Books. He, too, fears poverty in a community that does not support its scholars and clutches at the only resource at his command—his daughters. His one venture into the business world is as pathetic as it is horrifying, for his effort to assume the role of the American man only underscores his lack of training. His ego is so strong that he assumes knowledge in a situation about which he knows nothing. He is easily duped by con men like Moe Mirsky or the grocery store owners, yet when presented with the error of his ways, he finds solace in his religion, rebuking his wife for her lack of faith. The faith, however, also endows the portrait with a powerful beauty:

With his black satin skullcap tipped on the side of his head . . . his ragged
satin coat from Europe made him look as if he just stepped out of the
Bible . . . his whole body swaying with his song. . . . His voice flowed into
us deeper and deeper. We couldn't help ourselves. We were singing with
him. (16)

Time makes few changes in the old man's personality. With his wife on
her deathbed, he insists that his prayers at the synagogue are of more
help to her than his presence in the sickroom, but his suffering at her
death, despite its element of self-pity, is a reminder of the attachment
between husband and wife.

His downfall at the hands of the widow Mrs. Feinstein, who spends
all the lodge money and then sends the old man out into the streets to
peddle chewing gum, is perhaps overdone. Sara, seeing him on the
street, realizes, "How changed he was! How old and suffering! He, the
master—with the stoop of poverty on his back." (287) At the end, the
strength of the old man shines through as the daughter says,

. . . Suddenly the pathos of this lonely old man pierced me. In a world where
all is changed, he alone remained unchanged—as tragically isolate as the
rocks. All that he had left of life was his fanatical adherence to his traditions. . . . The look of bitterness faded from his face and he opened the
Bible, his eternal consolation. Instantly he was transported to his other
world. (296)

"Blut und Eisen."   Fine as the portrait of Reb Smolinsky is, the
stubborn patriarch clinging to the ancient values, even more of an
achievement is the portrait of the daughter. The technical problem of
using a first person narrator forced Yezierska to create her character out
of her own words and in the version of events that she presents. Yet she
was able to maintain a distance from her character sufficient to present
the faults of her virtues and the virtues of her faults, to show both the
child and the woman, to present her conflicting values and guilts with a
minimum of sentimentality or exaggerated emotionalism. Sara's de-
fiant courage—the "Blut und Eisen" that her father nicknamed her—
provides both the strength to save the family in an economic crisis and
to defy them in the struggle to achieve her goal. As a child, her concern
for her sisters' romances captures the interest that only the youngest

child could have. Yezierska catches a young child's wonder as Sara watches Bessie squeeze herself into Mashah's dress to entertain her first boyfriend, cries for her as their father questions the young man mercilessly, and conveys a child's fantasies in Sara's involvement with Fanya's and Mashah's beaus. In this way Sara's growing hatred of her father has been partly justified. Watching each of her sisters' chances for happiness being destroyed, then listening as the father preaches and criticizes them, she realizes that

> More and more I began to see that Father, in his innocent craziness to hold up the light of the Law to his children, was as a tyrant more terrible than the Tsar from Russia. As he drove away Bessie's man, so he drove away Mashah's lover. And each time he killed the heart from one of his children, he grew louder with his preaching on us all . . . He remembered the littlest fault of each and every one of us, from the time we were born. And he'd begin hammering these faults into us till it got black and red from our eyes. (64–65)

It is a child's hatred, but it gives her the courage that her sisters lack to argue against the father. When he complains of the poet's poverty, Sara mentions his former praise of poverty, saying, "Didn't you yourself say yesterday that poverty is an ornament on a Jew, like a red ribbon on a white horse?" (70). This hatred grows in Sara and the father becomes an epitome of all the frustrations of her young life. He represents the world of traditions in which only men were important; he personifies the Jewish ghetto which kept her out of the "real America." This rage develops as Sara herself grows into adolescence. And when the final insult comes, Sara's break with the family represents a break with all these elements; she is not yet able to separate them out.

Sara's struggles to make her own way are understandable here as they were not in Yezierska's previous fictions, for the rage against the father provides a psychological basis that on the one hand supplies the incredible energy and fixedness that marks her progress, but on the other hand also accentuates the peculiar childishness of many of her actions, her insistence on superficial elements, her refusal even to visit with her family despite her hunger and homesickness, her inability to become friendly with the girls she works with by sharing their risque jokes and simple pleasures.

With increased self-awareness, Yezierska was able to accept her character's faults without the need to rail out against external circumstances. She was able to show how this father and daughter, alike in so many ways, were drawn to each other and yet repelled by their insistence on the rightness of their own position. Both, consumed with the fierce determination to achieve their goals, would inevitably clash. Yezierska's handling of the main character is less successful in the later sections of the book. Sara's memories of her father's wisdom that come in the midst of their fight over her refusal to marry Max is too pat, and the description of her years at college exaggerates both the difficulties endured by the heroine and the charmed life of the other students. Partly, this distortion can be attributed to the fact that the narrator's vision is itself clouded, but Yezierska has not provided the correctives that would permit the reader to recognize that the distortion is intentional. The demands that Sara makes on her professors, however, seem believable as a search for a substitute father, but the adulation of the students when Sara wins the prize smacks of pure fantasy.

This sense of fantasy intrudes most strongly in the final section, yet there remains enough that is believably human in Sara's personality to rescue the book. Her complacent pride in her fine clothes and newly gained comfort is balanced by her recurrent guilt about her parents. Her desire to see her mother and to help her in her final hours sharpens the poignancy of her refusal to have her new suit cut in accordance with Jewish ritual. And her mature awareness that she cannot escape the ties that bind her to her father is justified by her new confidence in herself. She is finally able to accept the fact that he, too, is merely human and although she knows their relationship will always be difficult, she can see it in human rather than symbolic terms. Sara's love affair and marriage to Hugo Seelig, however, are the most jarring elements in the book. It is difficult to accept the fact that having strived for so long to achieve independence, Sara would so easily relinquish it or that she would so quickly find a man so perfectly suitable in all ways.

Yezierska's growth as a writer is most noticeable in the depiction of Sara. Images of a similar character had recurred frequently in Yezierska's earlier fiction, but they had all been fragments of a self. The young girl yearning for escape from poverty and Old World values had appeared in the person of Shenah Pesah in "Wings" and "Hunger," the struggling

adolescent had recurred in "My Own People," and the successful
college graduate is presented in "Children of Loneliness." But for all of
these forerunners, the influences that motivated the characters and the
results of their actions were left undefined. In creating Sara, Yezierska
could draw all these strands together. If she was not always successful in
welding these elements, she nevertheless provided a portrait whose
vitality stems from the contradictions and ambivalences felt by the
author herself which she was honest enough to admit and skilled
enough to dramatize. The conflicts and ambivalences are most readily
discernible in the presentation of the Jewish ghetto. The ugliness of
poverty and cramped living quarters is not slighted, but neither is the
warmth and liveliness of that world which could contain such helpful
neighbors as Mukmenkeh who could show them how to furnish a room
without furniture.

Put the spring over four empty herring pails and you'll have a bed fit for the
president. Now put a board over the potato barrel, and a clean newspaper
over that, and you'll have a table. All you need yet is a soapbox for a chair, and
you'll have a furnished room complete. (15)

Analysis

The pull of that sense of community is joined to the family ties that
support as well as imprison. The sisters may often battle with each
other, the mother frequently screams, but they are also there for each
other in time of need. Inseparable from these is the heritage of the
Jewish people with its innumerable restrictions but also with the faith
that sustains them. Both factors are embodied in the person of the father
so that Sara's alternate rebellions and regrets have psychological as well
as social validity. The choices that Sara makes are never perfect and her
guilt is never completely assuaged. Only in the ending does Yezierska's
clarity of vision abandon her. The philosophical and psychological
material which had seemed tacked on in undigested masses in her
previous two books have been integrated into the plot. The Emersonian
doctrine of self-reliance is modified by the appreciation of the reality of
the strength of old ties, and Sara's independence is punctuated by the
pangs of guilt. The isolation that could come from adopting the

Emersonian doctrine is not ignored and its psychological effects explored. Most important, the value of ethnic diversity, which Yezierska probably learned from Dewey, provided intellectual support for the main character's decision to return to her people. Unlike Sonya in *Salome,* who mouths similar sentiments but indicates no real commitment to them, Sara's actions indicate a merger of psychological and philosophical influences. Sara's return to the Lower East Side dramatizes the notion that "all get from one another the best that each strain has to offer from its own traditions and culture."[2] But because Yezierska had never lost her love of her cultural heritage, she is aware, as Dewey's words omit, that guilt would play a major role in that decision; thus, she has her heroine say to herself,

I had come back to where I had started twenty years ago when I began my fight for freedom. But in my rebellious youth, I thought I could escape by running away. And now I realized that the shadow of the burden was always following me, and here I stood face to face with it again. (275)

Although she regards her father as a burden, she is still charmed by the "mere music of the fading chant" (297) of his prayers.

Critical Reception

If the reviewers who discussed *Breadgivers* were aware of the greater depths and higher achievement of this work, few discussed it. Samuel Raphaelson in the *New York Tribune* saw it as just another version "of a theme of which we have grown weary—the story of a poor East Side girl who Americanized herself by sheer force."[3] The "invalidity" of the central character was for him the key flaw, but he praised the "tang of the minor characters who are sketched in." Others commented on the language or noted the skill with which the ghetto world was created.[4]

Publications geared for a Jewish audience were even less pleased. Yossef Goer considered it "a pandering to tastes of typical Americans which laughs at Englished market Yiddish and wants to believe America great and Judaism not."[5] He seems unaware of the careful control of language in the book, with the narrator's language changing as she grows, and that the use of direct translation of Yiddish phrases allows the American audience to savor the spirit of the language. The title, as he pointed out, is a direct translation of the Yiddish "broit gibbers" but the phrase conveys the bite and the immediacy of that language far more than would the American equivalent "wage-earners."

Yezierska had begun her writing career with the ambition to serve as a spokeswoman. Much of her early fiction is marred by the moral fervor with which she endowed her role, as she alternately manipulated events and characters to support attitudes external to the situation or created fantasy escapes from unresolved conflicts. In *Breadgivers* she seemed more willing to let the story speak for itself, to let the created character develop according to its own inner drives. The child Sara was based on Yezierska's own life, but the created self stands detached from its creator. But when the main character became a woman, Yezierska's need to justify her own life forced her to identify too closely with the fictional self. The result was to diminish the credibility of her heroine and to retreat into a vision of an impossibly perfect world with only the awareness of the burden of the father to tinge its Utopian quality.

Chapter Five
Years of Decline

The next five years saw a serious reversal of fortune for Yezierska. Although two more novels were published, neither achieved either critical recognition or public acceptance. The stock market crash wiped out her savings, and the subsequent depression made it difficult to find publishers. Her literary friendships were cooling off, and the threat of poverty which had so scarred her childhood threatened to engulf her once again. In her personal life she sought new paths to the inner peace and contentment that constantly eluded her. It was the start of a period of decline from which she would not recover for twenty years.

The lack of interest in Yezierska's writings was due to a number of factors. The curiosity about ethnic minorities, which had spurred the acceptance not only of her work but the Harlem Renaissance as well, was partially a passing fad that had run its course. Yezierska's fictions tended to focus on a limited range of plot and characters, so that the differences from one work to the next were indistinguishable to the casual reader. Furthermore, her treatment of the material was such that it tended to antagonize her potential audience. The newly arrived Jewish immigrants resented her critical attitude toward their manners, their language, their mores, while her condemnation of the actions by the Americanized Jewish community and Americans in general undoubtedly antagonized them as well.

Her disappointment with the New York literary scene is suggested in an unpublished story where she caricatures the very people she had been most friendly with.[1] This change of feeling may have been the reason that she sought out and secured a Zona Gale fellowship at the University of Wisconsin. From 1929 to 1930 she was a writer-in-residence there, but before she left, another novel, *Arrogant Beggar,* was ready for publication. Once again, she seems to have had trouble in her negotiations with her publishers, for in January 1927 she was writing to

Houghton Mifflin, who had originally brought out *Hungry Hearts,* discussing details of a contract.[2] Remembering her problems with them, the main point in her letter was for a "definite and comprehensive advertising" campaign. The negotiations, however, did not go well, and in February she asked them to return the manuscript. Her next communication with them gave her mailing address as Macmillan's. In the end, however, it was Doubleday, the publishers of *Breadgivers,* that brought out the book.

Arrogant Beggar

Although the novel is not as good as *Breadgivers,* it is useful as a comparison with earlier fictions. Reverting to a theme that she had treated in *Salome,* Yezierska was attempting to show how childish illusions and shallow values blind a young girl to the insights and appreciation of human worth that are a mark of maturity. Unlike the earlier novel, she was now skillful enough both to give her heroine's observations and at the same time provide the reader with a standard by which to measure them. The random touches of satire that had dotted her earlier fiction were now used to reinforce the plot, and the setting of scenes is more carefully controlled to underline the meaning. The honesty and freshness of her approach to her material, the intensity with which individual scenes are created are now focused on a central purpose. The problem now was overcontrol, for the book comes dangerously close to a propaganda piece.

Plot. The story opens with Adele Lindner, an orphaned immigrant shopgirl, as she is about to move from her squalid ghetto room to a Home for Working Girls sponsored by an uptown Jewish women's organization named for its chief benefactress, Mrs. Hellman. Adele, with her limited understanding, can see only the physical contrast between the two places. For her the streets of the ghetto are ugly with "houses huddled together . . . like a poor, over-crowded family . . . where even the sky was a prisoner and the stars choked."[3] But the world of the home was filled with "sunshine and goodness" (3) with its "white curtains, red and green geraniums" (11). The contrast is further heightened by the difference between the director of the Home, Miss

Simon, whose clothes are "so neat, so smoothly pressed out . . . Like a model in our show window" (8) and Adele's friend from the ghetto, Mrs. Herbein, the janitress, in baggy pushcart clothes, forever involved in the filth of ghetto life. Adele cannot yet appreciate the human warmth and support that she is so willing to give up.

Blinded by the glow of her own illusions, Adele sees the home as a haven that offers not only clean sheets and smooth mattresses, but also friendship and self-fulfillment. The sullen weariness of her roommate and the complaints of the other girls about the food and the rules confuse her but do not enlighten. The shallowness of her thinking is caught in her belief that the home would be a way-station to the only way out of the ghetto that she can then imagine—marriage to a husband who would be more than a working-man, someone who can afford front row seats in the theatre, boxes at the opera and dinner "in those elegant places with softened lights where music plays" (44). When she meets Mrs. Hellman's son, Arthur, he seems the epitome of all these desires.

Adele's inevitable disillusionment comes gradually, but she is so blinded by her own dreams that each event is unexpected and the girl is almost destroyed. First, she loses her job and discovers that instead of protecting her either emotionally or economically, the manager of the home tells her she must leave if her rent remains unpaid after two weeks. Miss Simon, however, has her own projects that she is trying to push and, taking advantage of Adele's desperate state, forces her into taking a course in Domestic Science Training given at the home. Adele, is, at first, hopelessly inefficient, but with a pang of guilt she compensates by spending all night cleaning the kitchen, an act which gains her the approval of Miss Simon and the board of directors. In response, Adele writes a letter of thanks so effusive that Mrs. Hellman rewards her by sending her to a domestic science school and giving her some of her daughter's cast-off clothes. Adele pays a visit to the Hellman residence to make the arrangements and once again illusions blind her to reality. Her assumption is that expensive possessions are synonymous with fine character, so when she sees the elaborate furnishings, draperies, and tapestries, she believes that they are indicative of Mrs. Hellman's greater fineness and sensitivity. The fact that Mrs. Hellman wipes away the girl's impulsive kiss is upsetting, and Adele is made miserable by the older woman's niggardly attitude toward the budget they prepare for the living costs, but she is still too shallow to notice the patronizing tone. Instead, she plays the part of the servile working girl, studying domestic science, serving as a waitress in the Hellman home, and secretly admiring the handsome son.

Adele's shock of recognition and her discovery of other values come almost simultaneously. She overhears Mrs. Hellman telling one of the other women on the board that she has been paying Adele less than half of what she would have to pay a regular waitress. The girl suddenly realizes that what she had been so grateful for was really not an act of charity or even kindness, but that, in fact, Mrs. Hellman had been, as she puts it, "profiting by my need. Even boasting to her friends of her triumphant economy" (21). Despite her anger, she accepts Arthur Hellman's request to work at a party for Jean Rachmansky, a young musician he is sponsoring, for she sees it as a chance to become more friendly with the man of her dreams. Although Arthur rebuffs her when she tries to tell him of her love for him, the party proves to be a major step in her maturation. For the first time she discovers a world of values that is not dependent on material possessions. Hearing the music brought Adele a "new sense of life," and the realization for the first time that "Life was not what you put in your stomach, or wore on your back, or the house you lived in. It was what you felt in your heart and thought in your mind" (128).

Doubly rejected by the Hellmans, her illusions now finally shattered, Adele can only feel hate. And this hate comes out when she is asked to address the annual open meeting of the home. Abandoning her prepared speech, Adele tells the audience her true feelings. Her angry diatribe accuses the supporters of the home of being hypocrites "feeding your vanity on my helplessness—my misfortune" (153–54) and calling them worse than Shylocks: "Shylock only wanted the man's flesh. You want my soul. You robbed me of my soul, my spirit. You robbed me of myself" (154).

Fleeing the home and forced back into the ghetto, Adele finds values there that she had previously ignored, embodied for the most part in the person of Muhmenkeh, an old, poverty-stricken woman who befriends the girl when she collapses in the cafeteria where she has found a dishwashing job. Muhmenkeh not only nurses Adele through her illness, but she also serves as a model. She represents all the virtues that Adele now sees as the fundamental values of life. She is warm and generous—giving not only her meager funds, but kindness and affection as well. She has maintained her independence by rejecting charity, has supported herself and her own tiny home by peddling from door to door, and has even saved a portion of her earnings to bring her granddaughter from Europe to America.

Arthur Hellman, who had been attracted by Adele's courage in speaking out at the meeting, seeks her out, but although he tries to atone for his past attitude by getting her a doctor, buying expensive fruits and even tending to the apartment, both Muhmenkeh and Adele reject his offer of money. When he takes Adele out to the elegant restaurant of her dreams and proposes to her, she can now reject him with the realization that in his world she would always be "smothered by their possessions" (212), would always be someone they would do things for rather than treat as an equal. Adele has finally learned the hollowness of her original ambitions.

Muhmenkeh's sudden death shatters Adele, but the old woman's spirit inspires her to make a life for herself within the ghetto. Using the knowledge that she had gained from her domestic science training, she transforms the dingy apartment into a warm, friendly coffee shop where the whole community can come, each paying as much as he or she could afford. When she again meets Jean Rachmansky, the pianist whom she had first heard at Arthur Hellman's party, the attraction between them is reawakened. He, too, has rejected the patronage of the rich in order to maintain his independence and has been struggling to support himself as a piano teacher. Their marriage provides an ending with all the strands neatly tied. Adele has her career and her sense of fulfillment; she has brought the knowledge she learned in the uptown world back to her ghetto world, yet has retained the old values from her tradition. She has become creative, supports the creativity of her husband, and finally repays her debt to Muhmenkeh by bringing the grandchild to the United States to live with her.

The Dangers of Organized Charity.   Yezierska tied the story of Adele's loss of childish illusion to a second theme—the dangers of organized charity, and it is her moral fervor that provides much of the energy in the novel. While her attitude was largely shaped by her reading of Emerson, it also reflected much of her heritage from the East European Jewish community. Charity had always been a basic tenet of Jewish law, but there were very strict guidelines intended to protect the recipient's pride and self-respect. The highest level of giving is when mere material help is combined with "bestowing of loving kindness."[4] Although conspicuous charity was a standard practice, it was based on the assumption that giving to others was simply social justice, the literal meaning of the Hebrew word for charity and was a requirement for every person. The recipient could feel that what was given was in part his due, and no one was ever regarded as being so destitute that he or she could not be a giver as well. It was considered a good deed to protect a person from being ashamed, and rather than waiting to be asked for help, the truly charitable individual would proffer a benefaction rather than wait to be solicited. Even when assistance was needed and no gift had been offered, it was customary for a third person to make the request, again sparing the needy one the pain. Often money was given as a loan, although there was no expectation of repayment, in order to ease the distress of acceptance. Much of the giving was through various community organizations to spare the individual the need to beg for himself. In any case, the problems of those who need help were considered everyone's responsibility, and either individually or collectively, they were expected to rally to each other's support. Yezierska's fictions abound with examples of this kind of giving, from Mrs. Pelz's assistance to Hannah Breineh in "The Fat of the Land" to the community support of the scholar in "The Lord Giveth."

Emerson's dislike of public charity was in part, as the epigraph to this novel suggests, based on the emotions it creates in the recipient. He, too, was aware that the loss of self-respect could embitter an individual, creating not gratitude but anger. He was careful to exempt gifts made with love, but at other times he objected to charity, for it robbed the individual of independence and self-reliance.[5]

Yezierska had railed at "scientific charity" from her earliest stories such as "The Free Vacation House." In *Arrogant Beggar,* however, the issue is treated with such passion that it threatens to engulf the entire novel. Adele's humiliations stem in part from the attitude of those dispensing help who treat the recipients as integers rather than people. The particular needs of each individual have no place in the factorylike efficiency that the modern charity purveyors demanded. Yezierska is also skeptical of the "Lady Bountifuls" in this novel who use philanthropy for their own personal self-aggrandizement, whether for the publicity they might enjoy in their missionary zeal to elevate the moral tone of the lives of the immigrant girls and to teach them "a love of honest toil and a devotion to thrift and economy" (107) or to soothe their own egos by sentimental pitying of the poor. But more than that, Yezierska suggests that the whole scheme of institutionalized charity is destructive rather than helpful to those who receive it. In her angry speech at the annual meeting of the home, Adele denounces the gifts she has received: "I hate every damned bit of kindness you've ever done me. I'm poisoned—poisoned with the hurts, the insults I suffered in this beastly place" (152–53). Her benefactors, she tells them, were "Feeding your vanity on my helplessness—my misfortune . . ." (153–54). Instead of gratitude, she only feels that she has been forced to sacrifice her sense of herself and has become nothing more than a beggar. Since Yezierska has all the girls in the home cheer Adele's speech, it is safe to assume that Adele's words reflect the author's position.

The contrast that Yezierska presents through the person of Muhmenkeh and her neighbors suggests an alternative form of charity that she finds preferable. The old woman avoids the Old Age Home, accepts no monetary help from anyone, not even Arthur Hellman, maintains herself barely above the starvation level, yet has retained her pride, and can say "God is yet good. With what bitter sweat I struggle for each cent I earn, but it's all my own—this place—when I pay my rent" (173). In this world the neighbors help one another out of love—Muhmenkeh tends a neighbor's baby, a friend offers her a piece of fish—help is given freely and out of mutual support and affection. While Muhmenkeh represents the ideal, Yezierska seems aware that such behavior is beyond most human beings. The compromise she presents is the approach that Adele uses in her coffee shop. There she has provided a comfortable, hospitable place where the members of the community can gather; she is not only self-sufficient, but helps others, avoiding the greed that would maximize her profits at her customers' expense.

Characters.   This basic theme is underlined by the presentation of the characters. The nonbenefactors of the ghetto world—here the "uptown" German Jews—are done with scathing satire. The focus of the attack is primarily in the overbearing pride of those who regard themselves as charitable because they support the Home for Working Girls. In a brilliant scene Yezierska presents them at a luncheon meeting, revealing their shallowness and self-deception in their own words. Mrs. Stone, who weighs 200 pounds, complains that the girls in the home are pampered by being given luxuries they cannot normally afford. Mrs. Gordon objects to the fact that shopgirls are buying silk stockings and fur coats, as she herself "smoothed her broad-tail bag that matched her made-to-order broad-tail shoes" (107–108). As they eat their elaborate luncheon, Mrs. Gessenheim suggests that chopped meat be served to the girls instead of roast beef. Their main purpose in maintaining the charity is revealed when Mrs. Hellman calls the newspapers to make sure that the reporters and photographers cover her group's activities instead of interviewing a delegation of foreign economists.

Only Mrs. Hellman emerges from the group as a more fully rounded character, for although she receives a far greater share of condemnation, she is also shown to be more generous in some ways. When the members of the Board are having lunch, it is she who says "I think we ought to feed our girls even better than we do. . ." (112) and who wants to prepare a special treat for them to celebrate her birthday; however, her real motivation is probably the publicity that might result. Yet in many ways she is more of an evil influence than the others because she meddles so directly into Adele's life with sententious pieties, niggardly gifts without even allowing Adele the privilege of returning affection. Although she herself does not work, she tells Adele, "Isn't it just as satisfying to the soul to feel you have scrubbed a floor more faithfully as to be mistress of the house?" (77). Even her response to Adele's passionate speech of righteous indignation denies the reality of the young girl's complaints, for the woman treats it as a sickness: "My dear . . . this is delirium. The girl is burning with fever" (157).

Miss Simon, the director of the home, is the epitome of the professional social worker more concerned with statistics than people. Her initial appearance, her professionally friendly manner, seen through Adele's innocent eyes, border on the godlike. The obvious hypocrisy of her monthly reports with their hollow platitudes, her concern for efficiency and deficit rather than human values, make predictable her cold response to Adele's troubles, and her decision to place the girl in the training school for domestic service, despite Adele's lack of either interest or ability, is self-serving rather than generous. Only Arthur Hellman, of all the "uptown Jews," shows any real capacity for growth and change. While his initial appearances are as impersonal as his mother's, and his rejection of Adele's advances are as callous, he is able to learn from Adele's passionate denunciation of charity. His sudden devotion, his meek efforts at help during Adele's illness, his proposal of marriage may represent too startling a change, but they are justified by the innate generosity of his demeanor.

In contrast, the characters from the ghetto world are presented as truly charitable. Even in the beginning when Adele's vision, and its presentation to the reader, is still clouded by her illusions, Mrs. Herbein and her son Shlomoh are shown as basically giving. Although they live in filthy, untidy rooms, the mother is self-effacing and has sacrificed everything for her husband and son. Shlomoh totally lacks even the minimum social graces, but, nevertheless, is burning with his ambitions to become educated. The awkwardness of his courting, exaggerated though it is, does not diminish the genuiness of his love; the ridiculousness of his having spent his last cent on roses for her so that he must borrow carfare, accentuates his generous nature.

The girls in the home are, with Yezierska's usual skill, sharply delineated with a minimum of words, and although their limitations are not ignored, they too have moments of genuine warmth and generosity. For the first time, Yezierska does not limit herself to the Jews; there are Italian, Polish, and Irish working girls as well, but except for occasional touches of dialect in their speech, they are undifferentiated. Their vitality, exuberance, their ability to forget their troubles in the momentary pleasure of a dance or a new hat indicate both Yezierska's sympathy for them and also her awareness of their shallowness. One minute they are complaining about the food, or calling each other "kike" or "wop"; the next, they are whirling together at an impromptu dance. Minnie Rosen looks forward to marriage as a way out of the home and concentrates her interest on clothes and her diamond ring, scorning the Tolstoy and Dostoevsky that Shlomoh had given Adele, but she is cheerful and friendly. Sadie Solomon is criticized by the other residents because her constantly gloomy demeanor dampens the spirits of the others. When they dress for the social, the girls help each other, even though each one may secretly wish that no one should look better than she does.

Muhmenkeh, the old woman who befriends Adele, seems, on the other hand, to be impossibly good. Not only does she take the homeless girl to her room, but also into her life. Living alone, she is proud that she is supporting herself by peddling. For her, the legends of the ancient rabbis have immediate relevance, and she offers herself freely to her neighbors, tending the babies, providing special treats for the children and accepting as freely the gifts of the neighbors. When Adele becomes sick, the old woman not only takes care of her, but spends all the money she has saved for her granddaughter's passage on food and medicine. Her wisdom and tolerance make Arthur Hellman welcome in her home, yet she can refuse his efforts to make her an object of his charity.

Adele and the Contrast to Sonya Vronsky. In the creation of the heroine, Yezierska's increased skill in character development contrasts with her more heavy-handed pushing of her thesis. There are many resemblances between Adele Lindner and Sonya Vronsky in *Salome.* Both heroines are vivacious, energetic young women whose ambition to escape poverty is at first focused on finding a rich man to marry. Both characters, deluded by their own shallow value system, suffer from the treatment they receive from wealthy people and both, after a period of suffering, learn to respect the values they recognize in their heritage. But Yezierska's novelistic technique had improved so greatly that Adele Lindner is more easily distinguished from her creator, her concern for the theme of true charity so important that Adele is finally a puppet manipulated by the author.

Yezierska establishes a distance between herself and Adele in a number of ways. Sometimes she uses another character. Adele's uncritical admiration for the Hellman Home is contrasted with Shlomoh's description of it as "ramparts of philanthropy" (22) and "the solid righteousness of its stone front" (22). Or Yezierska uses a satiric thrust to point up the girl's foolish illusions, as when she has Adele look up at the portrait of Mrs. Hellman which she felt "smiled down at her" and murmur to herself, "They wouldn't put me out with *her* here" (24). The author's ridicule of the objects of the heroine's admiration give the reader a clearer perception of reality than the heroine enjoys. Adele's irrational admiration for the manager of the home is tempered by the reader's knowledge of Miss Simon's opportunistic use of the young girl's misfortune to force her into a domestic training course. Yezierska has also made Adele a more sympathetic character than Sonya in *Salome*. Adele's naturally generous nature provides a sharp contrast to the selfish philanthropists who use her for their own purposes. And however much she wishes to escape her poverty, she is never totally unmindful of the values of the ghetto world. She may object to the Hershbein apartment, "so smelly, so dingy" (15); she may consider Shlomoh as lacking in ambition, but she also realizes that "His shabby clothes didn't matter. There was a look in his face that made me ashamed of wanting the comforts of the Hellman House" (17). She may reject the mother's poverty and ugliness of life, but she could also love her "because she gave up so much of herself" (19). She can also be aware, on the eve of her departure, that in leaving her poor room she was "leaving something of myself behind" (21). Even in her moment of wavering when she considers marrying Shlomoh, it is her ability to respect him and herself that prevents her from making that mistake. But most of all, it is Adele's courage, her moral indignation, to cry out against a wrong without regard to the cost to herself that distinguishes her from Sonya.

But in pursuit of her theme of rejecting professional charity, Yezierska is finally forced to manipulate her heroine. Adele must reject Arthur Hellman despite his obvious love for her. Adele believes that Hellman would never be able to see her as a person. She is, as she explains, only an opportunity to let him play Sir Galahad, always planning what "you can do for me, what you can make of me. And not what I can do—what we can do together" (212). After having Adele reject this love, Yezierska manipulates her to support other pet theories. Adele's return to the ghetto reflects her continued reliance on John Dewey's theories of ethnic values as she had learned them ten years earlier.

But the most obvious and least acceptable form of manipulation is Yezierska's decision to have Adele wed Jean Rachmansky. As in all of her novels thus far, Yezierska had created strong-minded women with the energy and ability to regulate their own lives and create their own careers, yet she seemed unable to imagine they would be complete unless they were married off at the end of the story. Jean Rachmansky is as shadowy as the other saviors in the other novels, his meeting with Adele is contrived and their growing love is hardly developed. Their marriage at the end gives the book the tasteless quality of a cheap novel and robs it of its potentially powerful statement about the trials and joys of a woman finding and making her own way in life.

Critical Reception. The book was not well received and a number of external factors can be pinpointed to explain its poor reception. The climate in America toward the immigrant had hardened, culminating in the restrictive immigration laws of 1924. The American public was no longer interested in the value of its ethnic populations. In addition, organized systems of welfare and charity were becoming increasingly popular. The complaints against "scientific charity" in this book went against this prevailing spirit. Furthermore, the condemnation of the German Jewish community would hardly have endeared the book to this audience which was, potentially, its largest source of readers. Whether it was because of these factors or the internal weaknesses of the fiction itself, the book did not receive many favorable reviews.

The Zona Gale Fellowship

The years between the publication of *Arrogant Beggar* and *All I Could Never Be* were increasingly troublesome and although Yezierska was able to forestall total disaster through a number of temporary arrangements, the loss of her savings and investments in the stock market crash in 1929 finally plunged her into poverty. The Zona Gale fellowship at the University of Wisconsin during the years 1929–1930 provided temporary relief. According to an unpublished manuscript, she had met Gale at a party for Glenn Frank, who was then leaving *Century Magazine* to become president of the university.[6] Gale, a well-known writer who had won the Pulitzer Prize for her novel, *Miss Lulu Betts,* was also an active political and social reformer, a former suffragette and a member of the University of Wisconsin's board of regents.[7] The fellowships which she had established were essentially for writers-in-residence, which permitted the recipient to take advantage of the university's facilities, but made no other demands. While at Wisconsin, Yezierska's interest in American education led her to investigate a new experimental college established by the educator and philosopher Alexander Meicklejohn, and to write about her own experiences. The manuscripts written about this period indicate that she was impressed with the free spirit and discussions which Meicklejohn was able to encourage, but she was less happy with other aspects of the university.[8] If the material is actually based on real events, as were most of her other fictions, she witnessed a strike by workers in the college cafeteria only to realize how her years of success had divorced her from the troubles that beset the workers. She found most of the regular courses in the college followed the traditional forms of lecture, readings from the classics, and examinations that had exasperated her years before when she had attended college. In one story she creates the character of an older professor, who was based on Professor Max Otto, a much-loved philosopher, whom Yezierska knew and liked.[9] During this time she was able to complete most of the novel she was working on.

In 1931, Yezierska, despondent about her precarious position, appealed to Dorothy Canfield Fisher, a friend from her heyday, who suggested that she move to Arlington, the Vermont town where the Fishers lived, and for about a year Yezierska attempted to remake her life in the small New England village. The experience became an important section in *Red Ribbon,* but while it provided literary material, it failed to solve Yezierska's problems. In 1932, she returned to New York City.

All I Could Never Be

All I Could Never Be was written during the years at Wisconsin and Vermont and was published by Brewer, Warren & Putnam in 1932. The novel reveals Yezierska's greater concern for formal structure and increased ability to establish an artistic distance between the heroine and the author. It is, nevertheless, one of her least successful productions, valuable partly as the most thorough exploration of the relationship with John Dewey and for the first appearance in her writings of the quietism and mysticism that were to become major influences in her later life. It is also another instance of Yezierska's ability to consider issues that would not enter the popular mind for almost another generation. Her understanding of the value of ethnic pride and her insistence on a woman's right to her own life are themes in this novel that would not be considered in popular fiction for many years to come.

Prologue. The central story of a woman's struggle to overcome the loss of love, is framed between prologue and epilogue. The prologue tells two incidents from the life of the heroine, Fanya Ivanova. Both of them involve superficial kindness and terrible rejection of a young girl's need for social acceptance. In the first, which takes place while the family is still in Europe, Fanya is sent by her mother to beg money from rich relatives who treat the girl pleasantly enough until they discover she has lice in her hair, at which point they eject the girl from the house, giving her, though, more money than they had ever done in the past. In the second, Fanya, now in New York and working in a department store, meets the cultured American lady who runs a club she belongs to and who invites the lonely girl to spend Thanksgiving with her. In her joy at being part of such a lovely party, Fanya writes an overly-effusive poem of thanks, but though she waits daily for a reply, she never hears from the woman again.

Plot. The events of the prologue set the emotional tone—the awareness and love of another, more beautiful and finer world to which entry might be permitted briefly, but which was closed for any permanent stay. The main part of the story begins as Fanya, now in her early twenties, listens to a lecture by a famous professor, Henry Scott, at a settlement house on the lower East Side. A man in his sixties with a noble head and slipshod appearance, he seems to the young girl to be "like Moses, Isaiah who lifted the multitude to the heights by the force of their prophecies" (9). Scott's message is that the mission of America is to end prejudice and discrimination against ethnic minorities. To accomplish this goal, he emphasizes the need of the immigrant to assist in the process. The role of the immigrant is to "accept with dignity and philosophy" (32) the slights which they experience.

When you have learned to look at your relations with other races in a broad, impersonal way, you have laid another stone on the road to the future where human beings will no longer be taken as members of a group for which they are not responsible but as individuals on their own merits. (32)

Whatever intellectual impact the speech might have had, for Fanya the professor assumes a meaning beyond the human; he is "the symbol of all she could never be. He was free of their sordid bondage for bread. He was culture, leisure, the freedom and glamor of the 'Higher Life'" (28).

Emboldened by his lecture, Fanya goes to Scott's office to give him her autobiography for use in his study of Polish immigrants, and hears once more his theory that the barriers that immigrants experience exist more in their minds than in fact. Seeking to thank him for his encouragement during the interview, she can write only one line, but receives from him in return a poem based on that line and an invitation from Scott to come to see him again. At their next meeting Scott tells her how the open, honest emotion of her writing has made him aware of what he has lost through years of repressing feelings. He offers her a job as an interpreter in his research project, and gives her money to live on so that she can write. Shortly after, Scott comes to the girl's room, takes her out to dinner, and they walk together through the ghetto streets. The old professor's romantic interest in the girl pervades his response to the scenes about him, and he marvels at the intensity with which the Jews experience every aspect of their lives. Although Scott is disturbed by his growing love and returns Fanya's letters, he comes again to her room to bring her a typewriter and some materials to translate.

Once the research project of studying the Polish community of Chicago begins, Fanya feels awkward with the other members of the team all of whom are trained social scientists. She is bewildered by their insistence on impersonal objectivity, on studying books and gathering facts, while she feels that "You must feel first what people love and admire—to know them" (81), an attitude which they dismiss as "emotional ecstasy" (81). Angered by her colleagues, Fanya goes to the Polish American Club. She defends the investigation team and describes her vision of America as a country still in the making which needs both the native-born and the immigrant, but she is at a loss to answer the man who asks "Will it help us to get jobs? I want work, something that will help me pay rent" (92). When she returns to her office she finds a letter from the chairman of the group to Scott, asking for her dismissal because of her "overemotionalism . . . her persecution mania, her unfortunate psychosis" (93–94). At a meeting of the group, Scott, however, not only refuses to do so, but suggests they review their approach so that they will gain something more than "rooms stacked full of tabulated statistics" (95).

As Scott and Fanya walk together after the meeting, he becomes increasingly affectionate, but when he kisses the girl, she sees her image of him as the romantic godlike creature crumble, and does not respond. He, expecting the passionate response that has marked her personality, turns away. At that moment the relationship has ended. Fanya realizes the depth of her love for the man, but it is now too late; all communication between them has ended and when she comes to discuss her final report, he has retreated behind a wall of work and insists she use the scientific approach relying on reason, not emotion as the way to solve problems. His final absolute reasonableness only arouses her fury and her realization that she is beaten: "She was miserably and humiliatingly in love with this man who no longer loved her" (110).

The second part of the book opens ten years later when Fanya, now a successful author, has been invited to address a college audience, to tell the story of poverty that had led to achievement. The story she tells them—of a book that did not sell, her eviction for lack of money to pay her rent, of her sudden rise to fame and wealth in Hollywood—thrills them and provides the acceptance Fanya craves, but she is still beset with the sense of her failure to preserve the love and friendship of Henry Scott. When she returns to her apartment in Greenwich Village, she decides that only by returning to the menial work she had known before her writing career could she wipe out the image of her ruined love and find relief from "the false life of fictionizing her experiences" (125).

Her experiences looking for a job shock her into realizing how much she has forgotten during her years of economic security. At her first interview at a factory, the boss refuses to hire her because he says, "You look too pale and you talk too smart" (128). The second interviewer rejects her because she is too old and too much of a firebrand. A third job is lost when a coworker recognizes her as a famous writer. When she finally finds employment as a waitress, she experiences some of the more unpleasant facts of the working woman's life. The cook, Frank, has the boss fire any girl who refuses his attentions. The girls are given a half-day off a week rather than the whole day which the law demands. Fanya, nevertheless, is excited by the fact that she has found companionship with the other waitresses and, watching the various people who come in, setting tables, carrying trays, she feels that she has begun to forget her lost love. At the same time she is aware she has also lost the ability to write, although she knew the world she saw around her was "living stuff that cried for a new Dostoyefsky, a new Tolstoy to be born" (174).

Appalled by the treatment of the waitresses, Fanya decides to help them fight for better working conditions, for an end to "the long hours, the small pay, the degrading beggary of the tipping system" (178). At the point where she has fired the interest of almost all of her coworkers, one of them tells the boss who throws her out. Back in her room she realizes she is still caught in the clutch of her love. She mulls over Scott's letters, all the times she had tried to resume their friendship without success, and then, finally, sends all the treasured messages back to him.

Even this gesture fails to bring Fanya the peace she had hoped for, so she visits a friend, Helena Hoffman, discovers that it is the Day of Atonement, the most holy day of the Jewish religion, and becomes aware of the fact that in her eagerness "to acquire from the Gentiles their low voices, their calm, their poise, that I lost what I had—what I was" (194). With this new knowledge she decides to see Henry Scott still once more. This interview is as disappointing as all the others, but for the first time Fanya realizes that she has never understood him, or even tried to understand. She has been using him, "using this man's life for her wishes" (202), rather than realizing that he was what his Yankee Puritan roots had made him and that his strength came from being true to them. Finally, she realizes that she no longer has any need of him, no longer needs his support.

Aware that she could not go back to the ghetto any more than she could go back to Henry Scott, she now seeks a new way of life, this time in a small New England town. The welcome which she receives, the neighborliness she finds there, the harmony with the timelessness of nature soothe her, but she soon discovers that the intolerance of others exists here, that the ragged children of the slum area are as unwelcome in the houses of the wealthier citizens as were the ghetto children in fine New York homes. Learning about Jane, one of the residents who has become a recluse, Fanya tries to persuade the other residents of the town to befriend the old woman, but instead of helping, Fanya discovers that she has estranged herself from the community. Finally, Fanya realizes that Jane does not need her help or her pity, but that she is "Serene in her isolation as the mountains" (232).

Epilogue and the Theme of Quiescence. In the epilogue life takes a new turn with the appearance of Vladimir Pavlowich, a former commercial artist who had tried to become a painter and is now poverty stricken and wandering from town to town looking for work. Instant rapport is established between him and Fanya. They have dinner together, but when Fanya tries to find a room for him with one of the local people, she comes into conflict with their fear and mistrust of strangers. Bringing him back to her own small home, she fixes a place for him on the floor of her living room. Lying in her bed at the end of the story, Fanya waits in peace for the unknown future.

Yezierska's increased control of the form of the novel shows here most effectively in the use of the prologue and epilogue which focus the reader's attention on one of the central themes. Although each of the three incidents deals with a unique situation, they are all bound together by certain common elements. In all of them, the main figure is a solitary outsider who has been permitted a brief entry into a brighter, more beautiful and richer world than she had ever before experienced. In each of the incidents the stranger has been accepted with apparent cordiality, but in some way has offended the sensibilities of the "in" group and has ultimately been rejected, a rejection the protagonist only dimly understands thereby accentuating the pain and suffering. But the difference between the two incidents in the opening and the one at the end is crucial. The first two at the beginning of the novel provide psychological motivation for the heroine's determined struggle in the central story to rid herself of those elements which she believes prevent acceptance and to strive to gain admittance into what she believes is the finer, more perfect world. In the incident at the end of the book, the woman has sought acceptance not for herself, but for others. Having been turned away, she offers to share the little she has. No longer determined to force events to happen the way she wants them to, she is now finally willing to remain quietly passive, waiting for events to determine their own course.

Viewed from this perspective, the plot of the main story assumes an emphasis hitherto missing from Yezierska's fiction, a treatment of the heroine that is strikingly at odds with her former protagonists and gives

us some inkling of why the book fails. Up until this novel, almost all of
Yezierska's heroines had been eager, energetic women who had refused
to let circumstances determine their futures, women who had struggled
and fought and suffered and fought again to surmount all obstacles in
order to achieve their goal. They had rejected small comforts that
might have distracted them from their main purposes, and even when
they were disappointed with the prize once they had achieved it, they
recognized their errors and themselves chose another route to success.
They were, by and large, women who were active controllers of their
own lives, and it was this quality more than any others that made them
stand out from the ordinary run of women in literature. This quality
was the one that was most frequently praised by reviewers and seems
also to have been most appealing to the author herself. Yezierska's
approval for this attitude is apparent not only in the vitality with which
she conceived them, but also in the generally happy endings with
which she rewarded them. In *All I Could Never Be,* however, the focus
has switched; the heroine when trying to determine her own way finds
consistent rejection. Only when her actions are described by the author
as passive, does her creator suggest that she may find peace.

    Yezierska's Interest in Mysticism.   In part this reassessment of
her heroine can be traced to Yezierska's interest in mystical and quietist
movements which had become popular in America particularly in the
mid-1920s, although similar elements had existed in American
thought at least as far back as Emerson. The transcendentalists had
based their philosophy on a theory of a higher reality beyond the
apparent, and both Emerson and Thoreau had studied the spiritual
writings of the Bhagavad Gita. After World War I, spiritualism was
given a great deal of attention in America. Works by Europeans, such as
Evelyn Underhill's *Mysticism,* were extremely popular and inspired
wider circulation of books on Oriental philosophies, such as Tagore's.
Numerous occultists visited America during this period, and groups
such as the New Thought and Bahai flourished.

    Yezierska's own knowledge of Emerson might have been the step that
led her further into these matters. She was for many years a believer in
Christian Science, whose founder, Mary Baker Eddy, had also been
inspired by Emerson. In addition, Yezierska's association with Zona
Gale may also have had an effect. In an unpublished manuscript dealing

with events just prior to her sojourn at Wisconsin, she displays some knowledge of her patron's work which had a deeply mystical strain to it.[10] Yezierska's own concern centered on Gurdjieff, Krishnamurti, the Bahai movement, and possibly later, the book by Hathaway, *The Little Locksmith*.

It is important to point out that while Judaism has a significant mystic element, Yezierska would have had little opportunity to have come in contact with it. The main body of these writings, the Kaballah, has existed at least since the twelfth century, and a major group of Jews, the Hasidim, has based its observances on mystical principles since the mid-eighteenth century. While Yezierska may have been familiar with some of this material through her father, it is probable that a full understanding of its nature was unavailable. The study of the Kaballah in the *yeshivas* ("seminaries") of Poland and Russia was carefully restricted to a few highly regarded scholars, while the more rational, legalistic elements of the religion were given the main emphasis. In part, this forced suppression of the mystic tradition occurred in order to minimize the false messianic movements which had brought only great trouble and disillusion to the already suffering people. There were many Jews in Europe who followed the practices of the Hasidim, but they were generally sneered at by the community leadership for the emotionalism of their services. And the Hasidim, with their general disinterest in the world outside, did not migrate to the United States during the period of the main Jewish exodus. (For the most part they did not come to the United States until after Hitler had made life for the Jews of Europe impossible.) Thus, Yezierska would have been familiar only with the more rational, legalistic branches of the religion. Whatever existed of mysticism on a popular level was primarily the superstitions and numerology which would hardly have attracted so keen a mind as hers. As one writer on Jewish mysticism put it, in 1913 "The prevailing opinion . . . seems to be that Judaism and mysticism stand at the opposite poles of thought, and that, therefore, such a phrase as Jewish mysticism is a glaring and indefensible contradiction in terms."[11] If Judaism had any influence, it was a force to rebel against, yet another way to distinguish herself from her father and his tradition.

Yezierska's personality, however, and her particular circumstances during these years might have been responsible for her turn in the

direction of mysticism. Her own spiritual restlessness was a potent
factor. As a writer she had, from her earliest stories, talked of a higher
life, an unfulfilled yearning in almost all of her main characters for a
meaning to life, even when they confused it with the grossest materialism. It is that consciousness of a *beyond* that is not simply for
Yezierska, but for all artists, the inspiration of poetry, art, philosophy,
music. And during the later years of the 1920s as Yezierska's fortunes
continued to decline, when publishers willing to publish her works
became more and more scarce, when the Depression destroyed her
economic security, her emotional state must have become increasingly
erratic. Always volatile, always overly sensitive to the least personal
slight, she bitterly resented the loss of contact with her "fair weather
friends" and her loss of public attention. In the manuscript that tells of
her meeting with Zona Gale, she also speaks in bitter terms of the
callous treatment she has received from people who had once been
interested in her. It seems almost inevitable that Yezierska would seek
out some new support for her failing spirits. It is only regrettable that it
fit so poorly with her usual themes in literature and instead of enriching
All I Could Never Be, it produced a quiescence in the central character
that deadens rather than enlarges.

   Characters.   While Fanya as a person dominates this novel more
thoroughly than any since Sonya Vronsky in *Salome,* she is less complete
a figure than Yezierska's previous heroines. Although she is described as
being vivacious and intense, the reader is more often told of her fiery
intensity than given actual examples. She seems more of an observer, a
spectator of the world around her, even of her own life. There are fewer
scenes of dramatic action; much more time is spent on thoughts and
musings. When we first meet Fanya, she is an auditor at Scott's lecture.
While Fanya listens intently, "her whole stored up vitality shining in
her eyes" (30) the active role in the scene is given to an old maid in the
audience whose "Breathless fervor now animated her starved face" (33).
Fanya's first meeting with Scott also focuses more on the man than the
girl. She argues with him about the techniques of sociologists, about
the treatment of immigrants, but it is Scott who is given the significant
speeches, as if Fanya's words were those of an interviewer trying to elicit
more information from the interviewee, or a good student trying to get
more information from a respected teacher.

   Scott's personality so dominates the next few chapters that Fanya
seems little more than a convenient robot. He talks of his response to

her story; he gives his response to the ghetto. Fanya occasionally punctures his sentimentality, seeing the swell of life in the street not as he did, "richness and color" (51), but as lack of privacy. The energy seems to be in the street people, not in Fanya; it is the crowd in the park that finds release in the music of the open-air concert, not Fanya. She is simply the one who watches Scott watching the scene. A few lines are given of her letters to him; two and a half pages of his to her.

Her passionate outburst when he returns her letters provides an inkling of the vitality that Scott finds so charming; her hunger for him when they are apart, her playfulness when they meet again are brief glimpses soon lost in the description of the man. In some way, she has become the wise one in the story, recognizing his sentimentality, his fear, yet appreciating his strength as coming from his faith in people. Her idealization of him, as St. Francis, as Christ, runs counter to her role as his critic and adviser on ghetto life. Fanya sees Scott much too clearly for the reader to accept the fact that she doesn't see.

Fanya's positive steps to make events follow the course she sees as the correct one are dangerous to her participation in the social scientists study group, abortive in her efforts to make direct contact with the subjects of the study and destructive of her relationship with Scott. Her arguments with the members of the study group only arouse their ire and lead to their request that she be removed. Her talk trying to explain the project to the workers at the Polish American Club leaves her only with the unanswered and unanswerable questions ringing in her ears. It is Fanya's rejection of Scott's passionate embrace, however, that has the most profound effect on her life. Although she has flirted with him in their relationship, she maintained in her mind the image of him as a godlike figure. When he reveals his very human desires, her response is revulsion. Although Yezierska does not endow Fanya with the insight to understand her action—Yezierska may not have understood it herself—Fanya had turned Scott into "her father, her Pygmalion, her god."[12] Any physical relationship between them could only be abhorrent to the woman. Lacking any understanding, Fanya tries to reestablish her relationship with the professor only to be met with continued rebuffs. She is hurt and angry by his response, but does not see her own responsibility in it.

The grief she feels for the loss of this love permeates the next two sections, and the underlying motive for her actions is her effort to forget Scott. Her ten years as a successful author pall in comparison to her failure to hold his love. And her achievements have not helped her forget him. The alternative method that she chooses—doing menial labor—does solve that problem temporarily but the cost is high—the loss of her creative talent. The sense of her being an observer outside the events is heightened as she surveys the bustling world around her which can no longer be transmuted into fiction. And the one positive action she takes to organize a strike among her fellow waitresses only causes her to lose her job. Her visit to Scott proves that her attachment has still not been ended, but it, like her attendance at the dinner in his honor, provides only additional rejections. The true ending of her emotional dependence on Scott comes when Fanya observes an old rabbi chanting the prayers for the Jewish holiday of Chanukah, the festival which is depicted as commemorating the return to the ancient faith. The juxtaposition of her last interview with Scott with the memory of her father praying provides one of the most powerful moments in the book and is also a key for understanding Fanya. The interview with Scott with its emphasis on death—his "dead monotone" (205), her "seeing him borne away in a sea of oblivion, among the fading faces of the beloved dead" (214), and the memory of her father with his message of light and hope—dramatically render the message that renews the woman's spirit. The division between life and death is blurred; the living have become like the dead, but the dead still live in memory and tradition. The image of her father and his words provide both comfort and inspiration and she plans to return to the life of the ghetto.

The failure of that action is neither dramatized nor explained, although it would have provided a crucial element in understanding the character of Fanya. Instead, the epilogue begins abruptly with Fanya's residence in a small town in New England. The sense of her being an observing outsider once more provides the dominant note, and the language used here stresses "Watching, waiting, expecting." Her efforts to impose her views on others by helping the old woman only cut Fanya off from the rest of the community, but the contrast to Jane's serene acceptance of her life and her excitement at the achievements of others, such as Lindbergh's trans-Atlantic flight, reinforce the growing sense that inaction, passivity, hold the key to the future. Thus, when Vladimir Pavlowich comes on the scene, Fanya asks others for help, only further estranging herself from the community. Her response is to offer what she has and, having accepted her powerlessness, she achieves an almost ecstatic state, "the tremendous peace held her in an ocean of quiet" (256).

Yezierska's theme of acceptance rather than fighting had the effect of making the character of Scott one of the most complex and fully realized men in all her fiction. While it is always risky to read Yezierska's novels in autobiographical terms, it is safe to say that this book is a working out in fiction of her relationship to John Dewey. The meticulous scholarship of Professor Jo Ann Boydston in her introduction to the *Poems of John Dewey* leaves no doubt as to the model for Henry Scott.[13] In addition, the verbatim inclusion of a speech by Dewey provides further substantiation.

Scott's first appearance as the lecturer at the settlement house provides a basis for the complexities that Yezierska was able to bring into her delineation of the character. His nervousness as he entered the hall, his careless dress, contrast with the immense importance of his role as a leading American philosopher. Warmth and humane idealism coexist with wide-ranging scholarship. Although Fanya sees him as a latter-day prophet, the readers see a man. Thus, when his ardor for the young girl grows, it seems a natural extension of his personality.

The growth of his love is presented with deftness. He is, he says, "growing stale . . . fatigued" (36), and the young girl's fire and enthusiasm, "the sense of wide, unshadowed brightness about her" (40), come as a spark of new life. His appreciation for her naturalness, her "direct, honest expression of feeling" (44), is a relief from the "many years of intellectualizing" (44) from his tradition which subjects "feeling to reason" (45). But it is his joy and his ability to help her to become a writer, his sense of participating in her development that makes the portrait seem so right. It provides the perfect vehicle for his change from the repressed Anglo Saxon into the ardent lover. His romantic appreciation of the streets of the ghetto feeds the idealizing romantic notions he has of the girl. His vision of her as the artist who is "eloquent with the beauty of the world" (58) further idealizes her in his eyes. Even his moments of hesitation are credible and give substance to the figure. He explains his going away because as he says, he is "afraid of myself" (63). When he returns her letters, Fanya says, "You fear to feel. You fear to suffer" (64). And though he denies it, he acknowledges that "My

cursed analytical mind keeps me running away from myself—intellectualizing—generalizing" (64–65). But his vision of her overrides his
scruples. To him she is "fire and sunshine and desire" (65). No wonder
then that at the crucial meeting when she does not respond to his kiss,
he is thoroughly disillusioned. He has created in his mind a passionate,
emotionally free woman; he has never seen Fanya as she really is.

There had been a number of heroes in Yezierska's fictions that had
been based on a Dewey-like character, and there would be others, but
here she would make the fullest attempt to understand the character's
motivation. His illusions about her emotional Orientalism, about the
romance of the ghetto are as thoroughly exposed as the heroine's
illusions about the coldness of the Anglo Saxon and the fineness of the
Gentile world. In what seems to be her effort to see their relationship
from his point of view, Yezierska has been able to create a more
believable personality.

The skill with which Henry Scott was conceived is matched by the
creation of several minor figures. Once again, Yezierska was able to
people a crowded scene in a few sharp strokes—the social scientists on
the project, the waitresses in the restaurant and the villagers in New
England. In creating the character of Jane she created a truly memora-
ble figure. A fuller physical description is given than is usual for
Yezierska:

Her yellow-grey hair, thin and straggling, was always uncombed. . . .
Joyless, griefless eyes, like dried out lake beds of sand. Her muddy face had
in it something shadowy and unutterably remote from the life around
her. . . . (225)

The daughter of a prosperous family, she had lost both parents in a
scarlet fever epidemic and herself had gone deaf. She had gradually
withdrawn from the world around her, yet as Fanya watched her, she
felt another kind of communion, as "her fingers seemed to draw into her
body, something of the animals' calm" (227). Excommunicated, os-
tracized by her neighbors, Jane has acquiesced to her fate, and "The
tranquil acceptance of her isolation lent a certain glamour to the ugly,
old face—the glamour of those irrevocably removed from the touch of
everyday people" (228). But when Jane shows her the newspaper, it is
her ability to "view the world from an impersonal vantage point" (231)
that raises her from a pitiable object to a woman of stature.

Analysis. The sense of ethnic pride is also given a new dimension in this novel. By presenting most of the scenes of the ghetto through the eyes of Scott, Yezierska is able to sort out those aspects which were valuable in her heroine's background, but whose worth Fanya had underestimated. The love of music and learning, the sense of community, gain new appreciation. Although Fanya's participation in distinctly Jewish life is given only minimal coverage here, it becomes a source of strength, a haven to which she believes, at least temporarily, she can return. There are a number of instances in Yezierska's fiction of a concluding scene based on a rabbi praying. Her choice here to focus on the ritual for the Feast of Lights with its emphasis on the spirit of return and renewal make vivid the sustenance available from the old traditions.

As a consideration of a woman's right to determine her life, *All I Could Never Be* provides a significant extension. The heroine of the novel is for part of the time, a middle-aged woman. The honesty and clarity with which Yezierska depicts the complex problems force the reader to recognize a struggle which had not received much coverage at that time. The scenes in which Fanya surveys herself in the mirror, recognizing the ravages of age and her difficulties getting a job add to the depth of understanding of an issue that has only recently become prominent. Yet Yezierska is still not so much a feminist as to imagine a life without a man. Vladimir is still another one of her heroes who appears miraculously at the end to save the heroine from a loveless life.

Yet, ultimately, the novel fails to live up to the potential that is glimpsed in occasional parts. Yezierska's strongest points as a writer had been in the vitality of her heroines and the moralistic tone of her themes. The denial of the value of fighting against events and the substitution of passivity rob Fanya of the most intriguing qualities. And while an understanding of others' points of view might have enabled Yezierska to understand her relationship with Dewey and permitted her to create a significant character in Henry Scott, it nonetheless removed the intensity which she derived from her former judgmental position.

Chapter Six
New Success

The Struggle to be Published

In 1950, when Yezierska admitted to being seventy years old, her book *Red Ribbon on a White Horse* was published. It was widely reviewed; the critics generally praised it and congratulated Yezierska on breaking her long silence, intimating that she had, during the past eighteen years, been suffering from a prolonged case of writer's block.[1] Certainly, the book deserved all their commendation for it is a remarkable achievement, a work of technical skill and maturity that makes it a rival to *Breadgivers* as her finest effort, but the reviewers were wrong in thinking that Yezierska had chosen to be silent. She had, in fact, been writing steadily, but the once-open market for her writings had all but disappeared. A few early works, expecially "How I Found America" and "The Fat of the Land," were widely anthologized, but they provided little public attention and less income. At one time in the mid-1930s she worked in the Writers Project of the WPA.

She had lived for twenty-five years in Greenwich Village, moving to more modest apartments as her economic situation declined. She had also lived for a year in Los Angeles and in 1946 moved to the Columbia University area. These moves, however, were dictated by emotional as well as economic reasons. Proud and stubborn, she complained bitterly and yet, apparently, often rejected the help her family offered, if she suspected it was charity. She worried about her health, dramatizing minor ailments into major crises. Yet through it all she continued to write, producing a number of short stories and an unfinished novel called *The Gilded Poorhouse,* which dealt with the fate of a group of middle-class victims of the Depression. She destroyed the manuscript when she moved to Cleveland. In addition, she worked on another book that would not be published until the post–World War II period saw a revival of interest in the kind of work that was her forte.

The root of the book lay in a short story, "What $10,000 Did to Me." *Cosmopolitan Magazine* had accepted the story in 1934. The editor there, however, suggested changes that Yezierska felt distorted the meaning of her work, and it was never published. She mentions having the manuscript of a book during the time she worked with the Writers Project. In 1943, she wrote Houghton Mifflin, offering the manuscript, then entitled *Sing O Barren,* but they rejected it, saying that they were "not sufficiently certain of finding a market to justify"[2] publication. When, in August 1949, John Wheelock at Scribner's offered her a contract, her effusive and humble letter of thanks seemed justified by the protracted struggle which she had endured.

The Auden Introduction

However pleased she was by Wheelock's acceptance, she had not lost her aggressive zeal and had sometime earlier gone to see W. H. Auden and brought him a copy of the manuscript. Auden had encouraged her and later agreed to write an introduction to the book. The essay which he submitted subsequently was reprinted in his collection *The Dyer's Hand.*[3] His was a sensitive reading of the work that attempted to relate it to the theme of alienation in modern literature. Wheelock was justifiably pleased with Auden's manuscript, but Yezierska, who was apparently unfamiliar with Auden's more academic prose, was appalled by what she considered "abstract Audenia."[4] While Yezierska's attitude was undoubtedly embarrassing to the publisher and to those close to Yezierska, it indicated that her approach to her own work and to literature in general had not changed over the years. She still retained the concern for a particular form—precisely ordered events rendered dramatically and in concrete detail which, like a Biblical parable, would render meaning without the need for explication. However fine Auden's interpretation might be, he had not paid particular attention to this aspect which Yezierska considered crucial. Yezierska was a highly intelligent woman, but she still distrusted the theoretical concerns of intellectuals which seemed to her, as she wrote of Auden, "shining words upon words, only to widen and deepen the gulf between his English gentility and my Hester Street."[5]

The Structure

The careful construction of *Red Ribbon* is a factor that is often missed. Since the book had been advertised as an autobiography, many readers, searching for a chronological narrative, found it "confused and disorderly."[6] But it was no more an autobiography than were her earlier fictions. In it are mixed real people and imaginary ones, real events and made-up ones. As in her previous writings, Yezierska has fused fact and fiction to create a new unity through the creation of a self that is not simply one woman, but a persona through whose life the reader may sense a larger truth. The events of the life of this created self, the persons of *Red Ribbon,* are arranged to underline certain major themes rather than chronological order. In each of the sections of the book, Yezierska considers one phase in the life of the narrator, each phase determined by the particular underlying hopes and dreams that dominated her actions. At the end, the reader understands not simply the plight of one immigrant woman, but of the many whose expectations met the same fate as hers.

Success as Material Satisfaction.   The first of the three-part division of the book covers both the literal and spiritual journey from her poverty-stricken ghetto life on the East Side of New York to the glittering wealth in the commercialism of Hollywood. It is a journey whose goal is security and peace through material success. The opening incident in the first chapter serves as an emblem for this journey. This incident, told in earlier stories in a number of different versions, is revised here so that its symbolic quality can underscore the main thrust of this section. In it the narrator tells of pawning her mother's shawl in order to get the money for a telephone call to her agent to learn of the $10,000 movie offer for her book. The shawl represents her last heritage from her European past, the last remnant of her identification with her family and its traditions. Moreover, this shawl, she says, "had been for her Mother her Sabbath, her holiday" (7) and it had for the narrator "redeemed the squalor in which I had to live" (20), and this shawl is the item she sold, as Esau had sold his inheritance, for little more than a mess of potage. Her visit to her father to tell him of her good fortune occurs as he is chanting the portion from Isaiah prophesying the coming of the Messiah, thus contrasting her father's living for God and His future and her own decision to live in this world for now. Even the train trip she takes through the desert is, by the imagery, a "rolling ocean of arid waste" (34). The narrator's journey then parallels the immigrant's journey; while theirs had been a physical leaving of one land across an ocean to another, hers was a spiritual journey from the Old World beliefs of her parents across an arid waste to a new value system. In every way this opening chapter has been constructed to presage the meaning of this section—the emptiness, the spiritual aridity that her choice would produce. This first image of America that she was testing was the most common of the immigrant's hopes that involved material comfort, economic security, cleanliness, good food, and clothes. The alien's wish and the commercialism of America merge in the concept that one is a person, that one counts, if one has money. And now she would have it.

In successive chapters of this section, Yezierska details the fulfillment of that dream and also the realization that it was a mirage. At first she is thrilled by the physical comfort of her hotel room with its tiled bathroom. Instead of stale bread, she feasted on Terrine de Pâté de Foie Gras. Instead of writing on empty grocery bags, and scraps of writing paper in her bleak room, she had a beautiful office with desk drawers full of paper and even a secretary. Instead of ill-fitting clothes from bargain basements, she could wear the smooth silks and gabardines from expensive shops. All these contribute to the narrator's sense that "I had pushed my way up out of the darkness into the light. I had earned my place in the sun" (39). When she meets the important writers at a party, she feels that "Success made people kinder, nobler, more beautiful. Only the rich had the leisure, the peace of mind to take an interest in one another" (59). Not only is this illusion punctured, but she also realizes that other important values are lost in the pursuit of money. In their concern for their own materialistic improvement, the writers she meets have forgotten the plight of those less fortunate. Truth itself is simply another commodity to be distorted for the service of money. The studio publicity man is interested in only those aspects of her life which he can use to sell her movie. Finally, even the stories she wrote, the message of struggle and longing of the immigrant to find a better life, are turned over to the caricaturist of American Jews, Montagu Glass, so that the comic touches the producers feel are necessary can be added.

Surrounded by a world so lacking in integrity, the narrator can no longer write.

Most of the events describing the Hollywood period were taken directly from Yezierska's life, but the denouement for this section was created out of her imagination. The narrator receives a letter from an old rabbi requesting funds so that he may return to Poland. Discouraged by the crass materialism of America, the rabbi longs to return to the land where "learning was learning—dearer than gold. . ." (91). The letter brings back the memory of her father and the realization that in the "ruthlessness of my ambition, the tawdriness of my success" (94), she had forgotten the verities by which her people lived. In a carefully constructed echo of the opening chapter where she had been too late to redeem her mother's shawl, she returns to New York to discover the rabbi who had asked her help has died. Returning has brought back to her the beauty of the traditional ways, but the experience of luxurious living has also destroyed her ability to accept the poverty of ghetto life. The search for security, for the American dream conceived in terms of money, has left her with only a dilemma—she is unwilling to sacrifice all her values to the worship of money, yet she has been too spoiled to accept the deprivations that a return to traditional ways would entail.

In the brief second section of the book, Yezierska presents another aspect of the American dream, another hope of the immigrant—that in this New Land every person would find acceptance and love; that true security, true success, lay in the contact of one human being with another. The opening chapter with its memories of past loves sets the tone for the whole section. In one, she remembers the hunch-backed fish peddler to whom she had confessed her urge to be a writer to make a living and at the same time her hunger to be loved. Crippled by these two opposing dreams, she finds an affinity with the old hunchback, and together they find solace in music, "the unspoken love of the world" (104). A second memory concerns her love for John Morrow, a lawyer for whom she once worked. The name and the profession are a mask to cover the true identity of John Dewey.[7] Their relationship moves beyond their workday association. To this "real American" she shows the world of her ghetto and her stories. Their feelings ripen into love. He admires her for her energy, her intensity, her fighting spirit; she is attracted by his self-assurance. For her, the two needs of her life—to make a living and to love—had been fused. But when Morrow tries to express his love in a physical way, the girl is frozen by fear: "old fears bred into me before I was born, taboos older than my father's memory, conflicts between the things I had learned and those I could not forget held me rigid" (113). Her response ended all communications between them, leaving the girl with the misery of unrequited love. She tries to write about her love of Morrow, but meeting with Zalmon the fish peddler, she decides instead to write about her love of her ghetto people and from that comes her success. The inspiration which this love has provided is perverted, however, by a new ambition. As a substitute for the feeling of one person for another, she now looks for fame:

all my hunger and longing for love turned to ambition. I saw a place for myself. I saw work. I, the unwanted one, was wanted. If I could not have love, I would have fame, success. (119)

The sham of her life as a celebrity eventually reveals itself. Dining in New York with William Lyon Phelps, a Yale professor who had become a critic of the popular scene, she is sought out by Frank Crane, a famous columnist, and Glenn Frank, publisher of an important magazine. Each of them has played an important part in her rise, but she realizes that their interest in her would last only so long as she was in the public eye. "As long as I was a rising star, I was in their orbit, and it was their business to make a fuss over me. At my first flop their blurbs would go on to the next best seller" (126).

Ridding herself of this false image of love also involves a reassessment of her relationship with Morrow as an infatuation based on envy. Armed with the strength these new awarenesses have given her, she delivers an extemporaneous talk to a college journalism society. Although she stresses the destruction of human contact that was necessary in her struggle to achieve fame, she makes no impression on them. Nonetheless, she feels a surge of real affection for the young women.

Success through Community. The third and by far the most important section of the book details the narrator's search for community. This aspect of the American dream—that in America when you need help there would be someone to come to your aid—that in

America there would be help for the downtrodden—receives the same wry twist as did the other illusions about America. Again, the tone is set by the opening chapter which describes the rebuffs the narrator received when she sought help from her writer-friends, the rejection from the writer's organization, even the failure of her efforts to work as a governess. Appalled by the condition of the unemployed she sees around her, noticing how "hunger and homelessness had leveled them all and dulled their eyes with the same look of defeat" (147), she realizes that their separateness and isolation have contributed to the horror of their situation. When a worker's march is organized, she joins the paraders and feels a kinship with the poor.

The major portion of this section deals with her experiences with the Writers Project of the WPA. The bureaucratic red tape that forced her to declare herself a pauper and apply for relief in order to get work amazes her, but so do the explanations of her friends as they describe the lies and frauds they had to do in order to qualify. The two people in the Writers Project whom Yezierska chooses to focus on represent two ends of the spectrum, not only of writers on relief but of writers in general, and at the same time shows both the stupidity of the bureaucratic approach and its ineffectuality. One, a tall, gaunt old man, Jeremiah Kintzler, had been the editor of a Hebrew weekly published by a Warsaw yeshiva. He kept clutched in a briefcase always at his side what he claimed was the manuscript of his major opus, *The Life of Spinoza*. The other, "A young Negro . . . with the calm smile of a young Buddha" (157), was Richard Wright, who was just then beginning his career. The old man dwells with intensity and sorrow on his past glories; the young man cheerfully talks of his unpublished efforts.

Within the project the narrator finds a social group that she longed for. For the narrator going to work seems like going to a party. At the beginning, under the management of John Barnes, a former poet, the narrator was permitted to work on her own writings. But the easy treatment under Barnes soon ends when he is found during a hotel fire with one of the women who worked on the project. Under the new director all former relaxations of the rules are ended, and the narrator along with the others is forced to go back to writing a guidebook to New York. Most of the writers undertake their new assignments, but old Kintzler refuses to give up his work on Spinoza and condemns the project as a "desecration of all that's holy" (176). Wright, on the other hand, accepts the work and, still writing in his spare time, submits a story to *Story Magazine*'s contest. Kintzler's anger and frustration find their only outlet in useless protests and letters to the president. His agitation only leads to his dismissal. Shrieking in protest, he collapses. The other writers, who have been waiting for their paychecks, are too involved in getting their money to pay much attention. Only the narrator is concerned and, rescuing his briefcase, she finds only "a mess of stuff, as if the trash from the wastebasket had been dumped there" (191). The few typed pages "creaked with the labor of incompetence" (191). Her sorrow and bewilderment at Jeremiah's failure are balanced, though, in the joy of Richard Wright's announcement that he has won the short story contest. She realizes that in one day she had seen "the beginning of success and the end of failure" (196). With the death of Kintzler and the change in the management of the Writers Project, the narrator's sense of community is destroyed.

Suddenly saved by the unexpected inheritance of $800 from her old friend the fish peddler, she decides to move away from the city to Fair Oaks, New Hampshire, where a friend from her successful days lived. The final two chapters present her efforts to find a community in this small New England town. The hospitality of her neighbors made her believe that "I could slough off my skin and with this new home begin a new life" (203). But when she hears the anti-Semitic remarks, and then watches the local Thanksgiving celebration, she realizes that she can never belong to that community, that a wall exists between herself and the rest, that being a Jew has separated her irrevocably from the others. Buoyed by the courage she has found in one of the women in the town, she returns to New York to visit her father, realizing, at last, that the security she had been seeking from America could be found only within herself. Each of the three sections of the book had traced out a separate aspect of her search for success—through material rewards, through fame and love, through a sense of community—and each had failed to provide the answer. She understands finally that she had avoided looking for security in the only place it could be found—within herself. Armed with this new strength, she looks forward to at last finding inner peace.

The careful structure of this book represents a major achievement and proves conclusively that autobiography was not Yezierska's aim. If the book had been intended only to be an autobiography, then the chapters covering her years at Wisconsin certainly would have been included.[8] In addition, Yezierska also rearranged the facts of her life to suit the needs of this fiction. Her stay in New England occurred in real life before her involvement with the Writers Project. By placing it after, she was able to maintain the unity of the sections devoted to economic and social concerns. In the same way, Yezierska's technique of introducing events of her life as memories permitted her to use them to reinforce particular ideas, to dramatize attitudes at a point where they would most be useful. By introducing the Purim celebration in Eastern Europe amid anti-Semitism and poverty, as a memory induced by the movie set, she could emphasize the promise of America of a life without fear. A more obvious example is the evocation of Zalmon Shlomoh, the fish peddler, during the second section of the book. This section is the one that deals with her contacts with individuals, with the search for love. Zalmon had offered her that and it had sustained her. The story of her relationship with John Morrow also appears as a memory in this section and that is, of course, the prime example of the search for love. It serves as a moving contrast to the superficial relationships she was having at that time with Phelps, Frank, and Crane. The fact that there are almost no flashbacks in the last section is also significant. It points to the fact that Yezierska manipulated the events of her life to suit the structure of her book.

The Writers Project

One of the most valuable features of this book is the record it provides of the Writers Project, vigorous and vivid in its presentation, pointed in its condemnation of both the government's bungling, the impossibility of a bureaucratic structure to deal with artists—as well as pointing up the failings and the foibles of the artists themselves. Yezierska's outstanding ability to create character in a few swift lines finds its best expression in this section. John Barnes, the first supervisor caught between the government demand for tangible production, is able to see the writers as the bunch of misfits they must have appeared to the military, and at the same time is aware, as a poet himself, that artists cannot work with the same efficiency as factory workers, that the measure of art is quality not quantity. His refuge from the insoluble dilemma is drinking, and drunken speeches at meetings capture the pathos of his position: "I was a poet. Now I'm a glorified office boy" (160).

Although the characters are chosen to represent the various types of people who worked on the project, each one stands as a unique individual—Priscilla Howard, the New England spinster, whose "shoulders shrank in fastidious protest at this horde of foreigners who neither knew nor cared that her ancestors had landed in 1620" (166); Bill Adams, the Communist, predicting the war to come with "a diabolical grin distorting his face" (163); Edwin Peck, the former professor of English, whose "eyes were sunk so deep in their sockets that you could see no color or light in them" (165–66).

But it is the character of Kintzler and Wright that dominate the story, and they contrast the two attitudes toward writing that were particularly important as indices of the narrator's dilemma. Like Wright she, too, had once been the young hopeful ghetto writer who would tell the story of the people, delighted to have a job and writing in every spare minute. In his success, she sees her own career at its start, the prize story, the book published, the triumph both a personal one and a "balm for all he had suffered as a Negro" (195). And she believes that he will avoid the mistakes that she made. "He would know how to take success for what it was worth and not become rattled by it" (195) as she had been.

In Kintzler, a character whom Yezierska created for the novel, she sees the self that she might become—clutching the fading newspaper clippings telling of past glories, still imagining himself as a young writer of promise despite his seventy years. For Jeremiah, creative energy had turned against itself and in railing against his own failure "he fought himself into frustration" (179). Like his Biblical namesake, he was the prophet of doom whose fiery words attempted to mobilize mankind, but unlike that great Hebrew figure, Kintzler produced only scraps of ideas on paper. His death was "an end of failure" (196) and in a certain sense it was the end of failure as well for the narrator who destroys her own unfinished manuscripts when she destroys Kintzler's.

The Jewish Woman

The narrator, is, of course, the main focus. While the persona here does not achieve the vividness of Sara in *Breadgivers,* she is a more fully rounded character whose life covers not just adolescence and early adulthood, but the larger span of middle age as well. Yezierska here was able to separate her author self from the created self, a detachment that gives a clarity of vision to the novel. The young Yezierska is not so fiery as earlier depictions, but the conflicts between her own enjoyment of economic security and her awareness of the continued suffering of others is the more clearly visible. Her disillusion with the life of the rich is more understandable, because the reader is not so totally entangled in the narrator's own misconceptions. At the same time the character lacks the sense of malaise that infected the heroine of *All I Could Never Be,* although the second and third sections here cover similar material. In the earlier novel, Fanya's work with the waitresses never comes to the sense of fellowship that the narrator here achieves with the writers on the project. And the scenes in New England are much more creditable, not a middle-aged fantasy of a lover, but a realistic reliance on the self.

The Emersonian note continues to shine through here, but it is not the naive optimistic reading of her earlier work. One achieves the goal of self-reliance here, as Emerson had warned, not easily, but with trial and pain and yet it was worth the fight. At the end she had come back to herself—not as some critics seem to feel to the self of her childhood Judaism, but to the new self which is the sum of all her experiences—of the search for security in money, in love, in community.

Critical Reception

By 1950 when *Red Ribbon* appeared, there were not only reviewers for it who commanded wide audiences, but there was also a public now interested in exploring more thoroughly the meaning of being Jewish in America. Orville Prescott called it "intense, emotional, extraordinarily frank . . . a revealing and touching human document."[9] Lyman Bryson found it "singularly moving, the disturbing truth about her own soul."[10] The most thoughtful of the reviewers, Robert Langbaum in *Commentary* pointed out that the value of the book is that it tells a particular story "of the immigrant, particularly the Jewish immigrant who having rejected his old culture finds in America no new culture to take its place." It presents, he says, "nothing at second hand, but only such wisdom as she has herself achieved genuinely and passionately through experience."[11] In *Jewish Frontier,* the reviewer recognized that "there was a universality to the problems Anzia Yezierska faced" and admires the fact that she never chose to do anything destructive, "the only person she hurt was herself."[12]

Despite Yezierska's reservations, one of the most perceptive of the writers about this book was W. H. Auden who wrote the introduction. For him the central issue in the book was the search for vocation. He called the book "an account of her efforts to discard fantastic desires and find real ones, both material and spiritual."[13] This right to a vocation he sees as the connecting link between her father and herself, while at the same time it was their major point of difference, since in her father's tradition a woman achieves existence only through marriage and motherhood. Auden not only located the focus of the novel as the conflict between the father and the daughter, but also the failure of America to support Yezierska's search either because of the commercialism of Hollywood or in the competitiveness of the American spirit. Yezierska's search is the search for a tradition to support her personal goals. For Auden, then, Yezierska's story of the immigrant became "a symbol for Everyman" for whom "the natural and unconscious community of tradition is rapidly disappearing from the earth."[14]

Despite the fine reviews and the new public interest in the position of minorities, the book did not sell very well. In part this could have been due to the fact that it was given only a very small advertising budget and even in those few announcements it had been billed as an autobiography of a Jewish immigrant. Readers who expected to find Yezierska's life story were bound to be disappointed; those who expected stronger Jewish content would feel cheated. And the audience who would be searching for stories of a woman's struggle to define her life had not yet developed. For Yezierska herself, however, the book would become a major turning point. Out of the maturity which this novel displays— the ability to synthesize the disparate elements of life, to order them and find meaning, as this book so clearly does—came new acceptance and publications, the more remarkable because they were the work of a woman who was now past seventy years old. For the next twenty years of her life Yezierska would be an active writer, finding a new subject, a new cause, energetic as ever, her moral spirit voicing indignation for a new kind of alien in America—the aged.

Chapter Seven
A New Cause

The last twenty years of her life saw a minor resurgence of interest in Yezierska's writings. Not only did she treat an entirely new topic—the problems of the aged—but she did so with a vigor and passion that had not appeared in her work since the early 1920s. She had lost none of her narrative skill and a strong sense of moral indignation replaced the tone of quietism that had predominated in her last novels. Her personal interest in mysticism continued—she added Alan Watts to her list of favorite authors—but she had also found new inspiration. In 1949 she had taken a course with Reinhold Niebuhr at the Riverside Church. Entitled "Applied Christianity," she called it "applied humanity."[1] As her words suggest, her lack of interest in the particular dogma of Christianity permitted her to avoid any sense of conflict with her identification with the Jewish people. For many years Niebuhr's thought would serve as a guide and mentor. She continued to use herself as a persona in her writings and to base her narratives on her experiences, yet she forged a new path for the discussion of a topic that would become an important problem in American society.

Book Reviews

During this period Yezierska also undertook a form of writing that was comparatively new—the book review. She had done occasional pieces during the 1920s, but now, for a ten-year period, beginning in 1951, she wrote fifty reviews that were published in the *New York Times*. She had apparently enjoyed working on them and treated them with the same care she gave to her other writings, but in tone and style they are remarkably different. The kinds of books she considered may have been due more to the editor's assessment of her ability than to her own inclinations, so no judgment can be drawn about her interests from this source. The light they might shed on her attitude toward the writing of fiction has been discussed elsewhere, but they do also provide an important clue to what she considered the role of a reviewer to be, and they also provide an insight into her attitudes toward Judaism and her sense of herself as a woman and as a Jew.

This difference in tone is the most striking thing about these reviews. There is none of the emotionalism or intensity that spark her stories and articles. The explanation for this may lie partly in her sense of persona. Just as she created an image of the immigrant girl passionately fighting for her right to be somebody and then both wrote and, in part, lived that role, here she created another persona, the image of the ideal reviewer as gentle, wise, sufficiently learned to make allusions and draw out meanings, but above all an appreciator. As she had written to Auden concerning his introduction to *Red Ribbon,* she saw the role of a critic not to analyze, but to appreciate.[2] In the bulk of her reviews, therefore, she takes great pains to find points worth praising. In one review she would praise a book for "brutal realism and compassionate power."[3] Another mentions the author's ability to "evoke the lyric feeling of young love before thinking falsifies and reason mocks it."[4] She was never dishonest, however, and she punctuated her praise, when necessary, to point out flaws. In one book she felt that the author's failure was due to "the way the author tells about her people, instead of letting them speak, think and act for themselves."[5]

Books on Jewish Themes.   A large number of her reviews dealt with books on Jewish subjects, and they accentuate the enduring love she had for her Yiddish heritage. She consistently universalizes their experience, however, seeing them as "timeless characters who speak for humanity in all ages"[6] or as "characters that are universal human symbols of the worldly and the supernatural."[7] Yet she is aware of the specific value of Judaism in their lives "that sustained them and nurtured the hope that their children and their children's children would have a better world."[8] In her discussions of the immigrant experience, Yezierska always seemed to point out the tension between the horrors of the European experience and the nostalgia for the communal life there. She also sees how a Yiddish background may have influenced the ability to write. In discussing the fact that Yuri Suhl published three volumes of Yiddish verse before turning to novels in

English, Yezierska says, "It is not surprising then that he has the ability to create and evoke characters that are distinct individuals, endowed with meaning and relevance beyond their time and place."[9] In the books that dealt with Israel, Yezierska made the analogy of Israel to America at the turn of the century, dismissing insinuations that one book of fulsome praise could be considered only propaganda, objecting to the lack of fire in another presentation, and finding a redemptive quality in the struggle of the Jews to "reclaim their homeland."[10]

Books about Women. Many of the books that Yezierska reviewed dealt with women as key figures; however, she seems less concerned with praising them as feminists than with their depiction of the general human condition. Yet here, as in her fiction and in her life, the assumption that women have a special struggle to achieve their rights underlies the text. In discussing a novel by Nelia White in which a woman is deserted by her husband, she praises the central character "lost, distraught, but still fighting for something that forever eludes her."[11] But Yezierska did not respond to specifically feminist doctrine. In her review of Yael Dayan's novel, one of the earliest of the feminist writings, which Yezierska compares to *Bonjour Tristesse,* the message of woman's rights, of the role of women as soldiers is not central to her discussion. It is as "a daughter of Pioneers"[12] that she wins praise and Yezierska's concept of a woman's role remained tied to traditional definitions. In the novel about nuns, she talks of "elemental instincts of motherhood, old and strong as life itself."[13] Her praise for Molly Lyons Bar David, writer, pioneer in Israel, Haganah fighter, is to call her "a journalist who is a wife, a mother and a generous outgoing human being."[14]

The Problems of the Elderly

As a collection these reviews have only minor significance. They are written in a smooth style, and reveal a fairly broad knowledge of literature, but show no particular depth or desire to engage in the more abstruse problems of literary criticism. Far more important are the stories and narrative essays she wrote about the aged. Yezierska's interest in the problems of the elderly stemmed, as had her earlier interest in the immigrant, from her own personal experience and those whom she saw around her. She saw the two problems as analogous, writing, at one point, that both "lack status and function [and] . . . are deprived of as human beings."[15] In her treatment she emphasized many similarities—for both groups there were dreams and expectations that were unfulfilled, poverty and cruelties endured and unnoticed by society in general, a few would-be saviors either inept or callous, and a population which had developed out of this treatment character traits that would make them difficult, even unpleasant, people. Yezierska could have continued writing about Jewish immigrants: American Jewish writers were coming into prominence and the next decade would see a resurgence of interest in this topic. Perhaps she had, through the writing of *Red Ribbon,* resolved for herself all those issues that had created the tension on which her art was built. But being now an old woman she found a new area that could spark her creative energies.

During this period, despite her age, her failing eyesight, and bouts of ill health, Yezierska's mind and spirit continued strong. Although her financial resources were limited, she lived as she always had since the Depression with amazing frugality. Leon Edel arranged for a few years to have her receive a stipend from the National Institute of Arts and Letters, but it was the honor rather than the money that bolstered her.[16] She maintained her own apartment, taking care of her own needs, supporting herself now with the few royalties from anthologized pieces and with savings from earlier days. Only for a few years did she receive additional help from her daughter. When she did ask for help, it was more often in connection with her writing and then she would approach anyone—a young college student who lived in the building, a stranger she met on the street, celebrities she read about. One such occasion occurred when, having difficulty with a particular story about two old women, she visited Joy and Marchette Chute, both well-known writers who had mentioned their problems with their mother in an article they had published. Yezierska had met them on a number of different occasions and they suggested that it might be easier if she told her story in a tape recording.[17] In fact, however, the tape is more a dialogue between Yezierska and the Chutes. Listening, one is aware of how strong and clear her voice is. Yezierska's mind has clearly lost none of its incisiveness. While the questions she was asking often sounded naive, they represent a deep probing of basic problems. In contrast, the

Chutes' responses indicate that they were unaware of the true nature of her dilemma.

"The Lower Depths of Upper Broadway." The first of her pieces published after *Red Ribbon* was "The Lower Depths of Upper Broadway," which appeared in the *Reporter* in January 1954.[18] Like her narrative essays of the 1920s, it was an issue-oriented fiction that contained a core of autobiography. The persona is an elderly woman living alone in New York and trying to survive on limited funds. The apartment house in which she lived once had been a pleasant building with a furnished lobby and elevator men, where the individual apartments had been arranged so that the rooms could be rented separately. A community bathroom and kitchen were provided for each group of five or six rooms. When the building is sold, the new landlords, "full faced men with thick necks and sharp, shrewd eyes," changed its designation to "Residence Hotel." The tenants expected improvements; instead an elevator was shut down, the furniture was removed from the lobby, and entire Puerto Rican families moved into one-room units. With so many people using the community kitchen, with so many children cooped up, forbidden to play on the street, with the fights and screams of babies, the place became unbearable. The narrator saw the Puerto Ricans, new immigrants, as she herself once was, the "newest victims of speculators getting rich quick on the housing shortage" (27). Most galling was the idea that such miserable living conditions could exist in an area where "all around us were people in comfortable homes, unaware of what was going on in this jungle" (27). With such congestion and lack of supervision came thefts, violence, filth. To top it off, the rent was increased. Her efforts to get relief from the city housing agency produced months of waiting, and the discovery that the building was no longer under rent control; the landlord could raise the rent as much as he wished. The only alternative for the old woman was to move. Here Yezierska had used a situation either from her own experiences or from one she saw in her neighborhood and had pointed up a problem in society that affected many, but had generally not received much popular attention. The old fervor, the tone of moral indignation once more had found a creative outlet.

"A Chair in Heaven." While the narrative essay was particularly concerned with the general problems of housing conditions in New York City, with men's greed and inhumanity, with the failure of public agencies to recognize the needs of individuals, it involved an elderly woman. Her next published story, "A Chair in Heaven," which appeared in *Commentary* in December 1956, focused more directly with the problem of the aged.[19] In this story the narrator, an elderly writer, is hired by a middle-aged woman to visit with her mother. The mother, Sara Rosalsky, a rapacious, self-centered, but incredibly vital woman, lives on memories of her past achievements, all of which concern superficial matters—her former beauty, the elaborate furniture from her Bronx apartment, the great bargains she bought at auctions, the tenement house she managed by squeezing work out of the unemployed workmen during the Depression, newspaper clips of her past philanthropies. Sara's greed is not only for things but also for attention from her family and she lived always on a peak of emotion. She is most proud of her charities because she feels that by giving money to the poor she had "bought myself a chair in heaven!" (553). The greed that marked her life asserts itself in her demands for the narrator's attention—"the passion of desire," insisting that the companion move in with her. Sara's children also urge the narrator to live with their mother, but their real motive is to discover what the mother has decided to do with her money after her death. Unwilling to serve as a spy to find out the mother's secrets, the narrator refuses. But she had developed a sense of kinship with Sara. She goes to see the old woman and finds her moved from her own apartment into a blank hotel room, shrunken, defeated, complaining to herself about the ingratitude of her children. The narrator sees Sara Rosalsky finally unmasked, "The unloved, unwanted child persisting to the end—naked, alone, facing death" (557). The mother's final revenge on her children was to leave all her money, not to them, but to an old people's home.

What is valuable in this story is the objectivity with which Yezierska presents both the mother and the children, each with their faults and their rationalizations, none of them really kindly, though all pretending benevolence. The characters are revealed in all their hypocrisy and self-deception. The mother is rapacious, using money as a substitute for love, hoping with it to buy affection in this world and reward in heaven, but the energy, the vitality that vibrates through her compels our interest and the narrator's despite her faults. The children, particularly the daughter, are more subtle, more calculating in their greed for money, the cold logic of their attitude chilling to behold, and yet so explainable as the reaction to the life they had led and suffered with this selfish mother. At the end it is the mother who has triumphed finding in death a peace which the narrator says is "the peace that had never been there before." The children are left with legal fights trying to change their mother's will. Only the narrator has learned from the conflict of the effect of greed on human relations, of the inability of time to erase the hurts of life, that pain and suffering produce people who cause pain and suffering to others, a chain that goes on through the generations. If Yezierska has chosen sides to any extent, it is to approve of the passion, the zest, the hunger for life which the old woman exudes. Although both groups are condemned, there is also recognition that their behavior is part of the human condition.

"A Thousand Pages of Research." While Yezierska was living through the difficulties of old age, certain segments of the American public were becoming aware of the problems. A major problem was the lack of useful work, lack of social contact, of long days filled with empty hours which dominated the lives of most elderly people in the United States. The social recognition of the problem had led in the United States to the creation of a number of "senior citizens" centers. Their programs were, however, essential makeshift, for little investigation had ever been conducted on suitable activities for this age group. During this period, Yezierska was involved in a seminar to consider this issue, and her response to that experience became the substance of her narrative, "A Thousand Pages of Research" published in *Commentary* in July 1963.[20] In it, she tells of a professor of psychology whom she had persuaded to meet with the older women she saw sitting on the benches of upper Broadway "killing time, waiting for death" (65). At the first meeting of the six women who participated in the seminar, they eagerly accepted the professor's optimistic prospects for the group. At the second session when his focus moves from their immediate problems to abstract theory, the group spirit disintegrates. The professor's lack of understanding leads him to make suggestions that they see as irrelevant or he retreats into academic jargon. The narrator sums up the seminar: "Our discussion trailed off into abstractions and the professor's words sailed higher and higher over our heads" (67). At the end of the year, as the professor fumbles with his papers, the women realize that their fundamental questions remain undiscussed, their situation unchanged and the key issue unresolved: "How are we going to live until we die?" (68). They had worked together, had tried to help each other and the professor to find some solution, but all they had produced was "one thousand pages of research," a sense of a year of work with nothing gained, the sense of even greater hopelessness than before, for the seminar had offered the possibility of improvement and in its failure they were now less optimistic than ever.

Narratives of this sort had always been among Yezierska's finest works. The moral indignation which she brought to social problems, the skill with which a problem is dramatized in the lives of a very few human beings, made her message come through with tremendous force, far greater than might be achieved by a more technical, factual essay. Her often stereotypical characterizations become not a fault but an asset, revealing how the problem affects a number of representative people in society. In this case, both rich and poor, Jew and Gentile, teacher and writer, domestic and nurse are presented, but each with sufficient specific detail to remain a unique person. And while the narrative solved no problems, it was for Yezierska of some benefit. The following year, the New School of Social Research, a university for adult education in New York City, began a program for retired professionals. A news story written about her attendance suggests a serious involvement on her part, but it is doubtful if she attended more than a few times, and then only for a social diversion.[21] Her energies continued to be devoted to her writing and occasionally publishing her stories and narratives for a few more years.

"A Window Full of Sky."   The next piece was published in the *Reporter* the following year.[22] Yezierska was now at least eighty-four years old. Entitled "A Window Full of Sky," it describes the narrator's experiences when she decides to move into an old age home. Poverty stricken, suffering the loss of control of old age, even to "the thin thread of saliva" that ran down from her mouth, she is contrasted with the cool, precise competence of the director of the home. The central incident focuses on the visit from the welfare worker, requested by the officials of the home, who were looking ahead to the time when she might need hospitalization or medical care. A small man, "self-important from his power to give or deny help," he only humiliates and confuses the old woman. While waiting for the final report on her eligibility, she goes to see what her room might be like at the home, only to discover that "the room I was to live in was a narrow coffin, with a little light coming from a small window." In contrast, she realizes that in her present home she has an irreplaceable value "the afternoon sun that flooded the room and the view across the wide expanse of tenement roofs to the Hudson and The Palisades beyond made me blind to the dirty walls and dilapidated furniture." Despite loneliness and fear, she chooses to remain where she is. In the end she remembers a brief scene from *War and Peace* in which Napoleon, leaning over a dying soldier to praise his patriotism, hears the soldier cry out, "Please! Please! You are blotting out the sky!" The image of the sky then became not simply a desirable asset, but a key image around which the entire story is organized, serving to contrast the deathlike world of the nursing home with the sense of life in the shabby room. The story is not one of Yezierska's most successful, for the relationship of the welfare interview to the contrast between the two ways of living is not made clear, but in her choice of image to protest against injustice Yezierska gave an intensity to the brief tale.

"**Take Up Your Bed and Walk.**" An immediate result of the publication of this story was an incident that provided material for yet another story, this one not published until the year before her death. In "Take Up Your Bed and Walk," which appeared in the *Chicago Jewish Forum*, [23] Yezierska describes a young theological student who had read what must have been "A Window Full of Sky" and wanted her to speak before a student group. To her surprise, he asks to come and see her, and her joy and anticipation are mingled by skepticism. "Why would he want to see an old has-been whom he thought already dead?" (162). When he finally does in fact come to visit, his presence lights up her shabby room and she feels rejuvenated, ready to start life over once again. "Old Woman! Wake up and live! Take up your bed and walk! You have work to do before you die!" (163). The next day the young man calls again, this time asking if he might bring his girl friend to meet her. For the narrator the visit becomes "a feast of communication" (163). As the conversation revives old memories, the narrator becomes increasingly agitated and overemotional. The sudden revelation of her torment, punctuated by the fact that her false teeth had fallen out, embarrasses the young couple. They start to leave and nothing the narrator can say—of her need for them, of the joy of talking, of a sense of friendship—will make them stay. The story ends with a note that accompanied a gift that the girl sends to the author "In hopes that others will enjoy tea with you as we did" (165). The reader knows, as does the narrator, that these two will never come again, that the moment was but a fleeting break in the monotony of old age, that greater despair had succeeded the old depression.

In the story the point is beautifully made. Youth's inability to communicate across the generations only sharpens the awareness of the old that they are cut off from the mainstream of life. But the narrator of the story is not exactly the same as Yezierska, the writer, and this point should be as clear now as it was in all her early fiction, even the earliest. For Yezierska, the writer, looked at her own life and transmuted the despair she felt into the substance for yet another story, and with her unconquerable spirit despite ill health, she went to work, as she says in the title. Both messages shine out of the story and the tensions between them make it one of her finest efforts.

"The Open Cage."   In addition to the book reviews, stories, and articles which Yezierska had published during these years, she produced several other pieces which she either was unable to complete or which she could not place. One of these, edited by her daughter, is "The Open Cage," which appeared in a new anthology in 1979.[24] The story is told by the narrator, who is an old, somewhat ridiculous woman into whose room a small bird flies. Agitated, the old woman calls for help from her neighbor, a woman who has kept many birds in her room. The other woman, unpleasant in many ways and disliked by the narrator, nevertheless handles the bird without fear and the bird responds in a like manner. They try to keep the bird in a cage, but the bird sickens and apparently is dying. The neighbor explains that the bird must be set free, and although the narrator protests, they go to the park, where they open the cage. The bird revives and flies away. What makes the story effective is the use of the image of the bird in juxtaposition with the figure of the old woman. The old woman's situation in the rooming house is described in all its unpleasantness, but not until the last line, "We were leaving the bird behind us, and we were going back into our cage," is the parallel specifically mentioned. The only significant change the daughter made in editing this story was to remove a paragraph that followed this line, leaving it as a finale that would underscore the meaning. But the story is not a depressing one, for as the narrator watches the bird fly free she rejoices in its "power to go beyond me." The bird is then a part of herself that can overcome itself.

Unpublished Stories. One story among her unpublished manuscripts is about a man in an old age home. Yezierska had worked as a volunteer in the home for a period of time, and the incident is based on a character she met there.[25] The old man had never read a book in his life because he was always working. Now in his old age he is bored. The librarian in the home suggests he read, and his discovery of this new world revives him. After that he is never without a book. Another story she was working on up to the end centered around a dream of a door made of faces.[26] Although it would probably have been further revised if Yezierska had had the energy and the time, it represents a very moving expression of an old person's attitude toward death. It describes an old, blind woman who has a strange dream that recalls to her mind the memories of her father, who condemned her wanting to be a writer and called her "an ignorant red-headed fool" and her "wanting to ask his beard who is responsible for my wild hair." Most of the separate incidents she attaches to the dream deal with the problems of the inability to communicate, of a fear of silence. She mentions a time she visited a niece against her will because she could not tell her that she did not want to go; a hairdresser who cut her hair so badly but to whom she could say nothing; a memory of her mother dying and only the eyes to communicate with. But the silences that had haunted her now no longer seem so threatening: "Silence that I had fled all my life. I knew even in silence that this was the call of death. Death now seemed a friend."

Difficulty came when she began losing her sight sometime in the 1960s. Nevertheless, she visited her daughter in Indiana and, indomitable as ever, gave a speech to a writing class at Purdue and another for a local Jewish organization. In 1964, she moved to Cleveland, where her daughter lived. Her physical state was deteriorating and she spent a month in a convalescent hospital. Not until more than four years later was she finally placed in a home. Her mind still clear, she made friends with the janitor, with whom she discussed the poetry of Langston

Hughes. The last year and a half of her life were spent in California, and even there, almost blind, physically quite ill, she had plans to work at the Judah Magnes Museum. She died in 1970. Although the obituary covered the high points of her unusually varied life, there was so much more to tell.

Chapter Eight
Conclusion

Anzia Yezierska's career spanned more than fifty-five years. During that time she published five full-length works, two volumes of short pieces, as well as numerous stories, essays, and book reviews. The best of her writing dealt with two main themes—the plight of the young immigrant Jewish woman and the problems of the elderly in American society. To both, she brought a prophet's zeal for pointing out injustice at a time when the difficulties were only dimly appreciated.

Her early writings dealt primarily with life of the Jewish immigrants on the Lower East Side of New York. Her skill in capturing a scene and creating a personality in a few vivid strokes was combined with acute perception of the dilemmas that confronted these people. Focusing primarily on women, she showed their struggles against poverty and menial labor, their efforts to gain an education, their longing to carve out decent lives for themselves. Aware of the conflicts and confusions they faced, she was able to show both the warmth and supportiveness of the traditional community as well as the obstacles it placed in the path of women. At the same time she was aware of dangers they faced from the American world with its coldness and indifference. Unhappy choices between material success and spiritual values, between filial duty and personal achievement, between ambition and personal integrity are dramatized with passion and insight. Although she found it useful to play the role of the ignorant immigrant girl who was frequently her heroine, it was her education, and particularly her association with John Dewey, that inspired her and gave her the insight to recreate the world of the immigrant. Because she retained her emotional ties to the world of her origins, she was able to assess more accurately the American world to which these immigrants aspired. Often Yezierska's sense of moral indignation or her desire for a happy ending overrode her awareness of the complexities of her material, but at her best, in *Breadgivers* and in *Red Ribbon on a White Horse,* she treated these people and their situation with compassion and understanding. When Yezierska was more than seventy years old she found a new cause on which to focus—the mistreatment of the elderly. With the same passion and energy that had marked her treatment of immigrant women, she condemned the cruelties of our society. Whether she was dealing with money-grubbing landlords or insensitive academics, she was quick to point up the injuries sustained by their victims. Nor had she lost her inability to recognize the less than admirable qualities of her subjects. Although her silence over an almost twenty-year period was due more to a failure to find publishers than to a waning of her writing, this new theme stimulated her to a new period of creativity. At her death she left a number of manuscripts that pursued different aspects of this theme.

Both of these themes are prominent issues in our world, and it is a measure of Yezierska's achievement that she was in the vanguard of those who appreciated their significance. But it is unwise to overestimate Yezierska's contribution. Despite her skill in creating scenes and characters, she lacked the ability to create fully rounded characters or plots that ended as honestly as they had begun. Moral indignation often interfered with aesthetic values. Yet, Yezierska's contribution has deepened and broadened American literature.

Notes and References

Chapter One

1. Although most of Yezierska's fiction is based on autobiographical materials, and despite the fact that she gave frequent interviews, there is little precise information about many facts of Yezierska's life, such as the date of her birth or the date the family arrived in New York. These details may have been forgotten, but even if remembered, Yezierska "revised" them to suit her need to appear as the spokeswoman for her group.

2. *Hungry Hearts* (Boston, 1920). p. 261.

3. Mary Antin, *This Promised Land* (Boston: Houghton Mifflin, 1912).

4. Emma Lazarus, who visited the immigrants at Castle Garden and Ward's Island (the predecessor to Ellis Island), described their pathetic state and was instrumental in securing help for them. See *An Epistle to the Hebrews* (New York: The Press of Philip Cowen, 1900), pp. 43–46, 64–68. See also Eve Merriam's biography of Lazarus, *The Voice of Liberty* (New York: Farrar Straus, 1959), pp. 85–101.

5. Jacob Riis, *How the Other Half Lives* (New York: Sagamore Press, 1957), p. 80.

6. John Higham, *Send These to Me* (New York: Atheneum, 1975), p. 5.

7. Mark Zborewski and Elizabeth Herzog, *Life Is with People* (New York, Schocken Books 1952), p. 116.

8. Ibid., p. 105.

9. In the 1880s, over 200,000 East European Jews came to the United States; in the 1890s, over 300,000. From 1900 to 1914, 1.5 million more arrived. Moses Rischin, *The Promised City* (New York, 1962), p. 20.

10. Rebekkah Kohut described the difficulty she had persuading other scholarly Jews of the necessity of going to work. *My Portion* (New York: T. Seltzer, 1925), pp. 178–79.

11. "An Immigrant Speaks," *Good Housekeeping,* June 1920, p. 21.

12. "We Can Change Our Moses But Not Our Noses," Manuscript, TS, Anzia Yezierska Papers, Boston University Library.

13. Barbara Wertheimer, *We Were There* (New York: Pantheon, 1977).

14. Charlotte Baum, Paula Hyman, and Sonya Michel, *The Jewish Woman in America* (New York, 1976), p. 5.

15. W. Adolphe Roberts, "My Ambitions at 21 and What Became of Them—III, Anzia Yezierska," *American Hebrew* 25 (August 1922):342.

16. Manuscript, TS. Louise Henriksen Papers.

17. A full discussion of this relationship is presented by Jo Ann Boyston in her Introduction to *The Poems of John Dewey* (Carbondale: Southern Illinois University Press), pp. xxiii–xivii.

18. Roberts, p. 342.

19. The poem, "Generations of stifled words. . . ," appeared in *All I Could Never Be* (New York, 1932). It is probably the same poem that Yezierska was referring to in her letters to Ferris Greenslet, her editor at Houghton Mifflin. She first mentioned a poem she would like to include in her book of short stories (3 April 1920) and then asked for its return because, she wrote, "I must first get Prof. Dewey's permission to use it in any way." 20 April 1920. Houghton Mifflin Records, Harvard University Library. The second poem, "I arise from a long, long night. . . ," appeared in a slightly different version from the one in the Dewey collection in *Red Ribbon on a White Horse* (New York: Charles Scribner's Sons, 1950).

20. Before meeting Dewey, Yezierska had published one story, "The Free Vacation House," *Forum,* December 1915, pp. 706–14. After their meeting and before she won the O. Henry Prize, she published three stories which contain Dewey-like characters.

21. Roberts, p. 342.

22. J. Christopher Eisele, "John Dewey and the Immigrants," *History of Education Quarterly,* Spring 1975, p. 70.

23. Quoted by Eisele, p. 71.

24. John Dewey, "Nationalizing Education," *Addresses and Proceedings, National Education Association,* 1916, pp. 183–189.

25. Ralph Waldo Emerson, "Self Reliance," *Essays, First Series* (Boston: Houghton Mifflin, 1946), pp. 46–50.

26. John H. Randall, *The Making of the Modern Mind* (Boston: Houghton Mifflin, 1926), pp. 420–29.

27. Yezierska reviewed Dewey's *Democracy and Education* in "Prophets of Democracy," *Bookman,* February 1921, p. 497. She wrote, "Professor Dewey's style lacks flesh and blood. It lacks that warm personal touch that would enable his readers to get close to him."

Chapter Two

1. In a letter to Ferris Greenslet, Yezierska wrote, "Please do not omit Soap and Water. This was the first thing that I tried to write and it's more real to me than the other stories." 20 April 1920. Houghton Mifflin Records.

This story appears in *Hungry Hearts* (Boston, 1920), pp. 166–77. All subsequent references to Yezierska's published writings will be indicated by page numbers in the text.

2. The story, "My Own People," was apparently part of a novel of the same name which Yezierska had, as she wrote Greenslet, "broken up into short stories as I needed the money." 12 June 1920. Houghton Mifflin Records.

3. Abraham Cahan, *The Rise of David Levinsky* (New York: Harper & Bros., 1917).

4. Edward J. O'Brien, *The Advance of the Short Story* (New York, Dodd Mead & Co., 1923), p. 217.

5. *Book Review Digest* 26 (1920):581.

6. *Dial*, 21 January 1921, p. 100.

7. *Bookman*, February 1921, p. 551.

8. *Nation*, 26 January 1921, p. 122.

9. *New York Tribune*, 16 January 1921, p. 9.

10. *New York Times*, 5 December 1920, p. 18.

Chapter Three

1. On 28 April 1921, Houghton Mifflin sent Yezierska a report that 3,500 copies of her book had been sold and that royalties of $260.95 had been earned. Houghton Mifflin Records.

2. Anzia Yezierska to Amy Lowell, 9 December 1920. Papers of Amy Lowell, Harvard University Library.

3. See letters to Houghton Mifflin of 2 November 1920, 12 December 1920, 9 January 1921, 17 March 1921. Houghton Mifflin Records.

4. Frank Crane, *New York Journal American*, December 12, 1920.

5. Ibid., p. 14.

6. Yezierska to Houghton Mifflin, 17 December 1920.

7. On 31 December 1920 Yezierska wrote that the "contract with Goldwyn was still pending" and that she expected "to sign with Fox." Houghton Mifflin Records.

8. "An Immigrant Speaks," *Good Housekeeping*, June 1920, pp. 20–22.

9. *Red Ribbon on a White Horse*, p. 69.

10. Edythe H. Browne, "A Hungry Heart," *Bookman*, September 1923–February 1924, p. 270.

11. Examples of her heavily reworked manuscripts can be seen in an early version, "Shut Out," TS Manuscript Division, New York Public Library, and in later manuscripts in the Louise Henriksen collection.

12. "Mostly About Myself," in *Children of Loneliness* (New York, 1923), pp. 10–11.

13. Houghton Mifflin to Yezierska, 8 November 1921.

14. Yezierska to Houghton Mifflin, 10 December 1923.

15. The headline in the *New York Times* read, "J. G. Phelps Stokes to Wed Young Jewess," 6 April 1905, pp. 1, 6. On 21 June 1905, the wedding announcement appeared.

16. Rose Pastor Stokes was arrested in Springfield, Massachusetts, on 22 March 1918, and again in Willow Springs, Missouri, 24 March 1918. She was tried and convicted 24 May 1918. See the *New York Times* for these dates. She was a member of the IWW and in 1920 announced that she was considering running for Congress as the candidate for the Communist party.

17. Oscar Wilde, *Salome* (London: J. Lane, 1906).

18. *Salome of the Tenements* (New York, 1923), p. 163.

19. Charles C. Walcutt, *American Literary Naturalism* (Minneapolis: University of Minnesota Press, 1956), provides a clear definition of this aspect of American literature.

20. See, for example, Scott Nearing, "A Depraved Spirit," *Nation,* 6 June 1923, pp. 674–75; and review in the *American Hebrew,* 2 February 1923, p. 420.

21. W. Adolphe Roberts, "Hungry Souls," *New York Tribune,* 17 December 1922, p. 26.

22. James Harvey Robinson, "A Stormy Romance of the Ghetto," *Literary Digest International Book Review,* February 1923, pp. 14, 66.

23. Henry Goodman, "What Anzia Yezierska Doesn't Know About East Side Fills Two Books," *Forward,* 25 November 1923, English Page. Later, Alter Brody would raise the same charges against *Breadgivers;* see "Yiddish in American Fiction," *American Mercury,* February 1926, pp. 205–207.

Chapter Four

1. *Breadgivers* (New York, 1925) p. 8.

2. John Dewey, quoted by Eisele, p. 70.

3. *New York Tribune,* 25 October 1925, p. 20.

4. William Lyons Phelps continued to be laudatory: *International Book Review,* October 1925, p. 719; and Samuel Raphaelson praised the use of dialect: *New York Tribune,* 25 October 1925, p. 20, but the book was criticized in the *Literary Review,* 5 September 1925, p. 2, and in the *Saturday Review of Literature,* 10 October 1925, p. 2.

5. Yossef Goer, "Her One Virtue," *Menorah Journal,* February 1926, pp. 105–108.

Chapter Five

1. "Saint in Cellophane," TS, Yezierska Papers, Boston University Library.

2. In a letter to Yezierska dated 19 January 1927, Houghton Mifflin discussed terms of a possible contract for *Arrogant Beggar*. Several letters were exchanged and on 11 February Yezierska wrote asking for the return of the manuscript. Houghton Mifflin Records.

3. *Arrogant Beggar* (New York, 1929). p. 12.

4. Zberowski, p. 194.

5. In his essay on "Self-Reliance" Emerson wrote: "I tell thee, thou foolish philanthropist, that I grudge the dollar, the dime, the cent I give to such men as do not belong to me and to whom by all spiritual affinity I am bought and sold; for them I will go to prison if need be; but your miscellaneous popular charities; the education at college of fools; the building of meetinghouses to the vain and to which many now stand; alms to sots, and the thousand-fold Relief Societies;—though I confess with shame I sometimes succomb and give the dollar, it is a wicked dollar, which by and by I shall have the manhood to withhold." *Essays, First Series,* p. 52.

6. "Saint in Cellophane," TS. Yezierska papers.

7. Harold P. Simonson, *Zona Gale* (New York: Twayne Publishers, Inc., 1962).

8. The five chapters, numbered for inclusion in *Red Ribbon,* were removed before submitting the manuscript to Scribner's. They are now in the Yezierska papers, Boston University Library.

9. The character, Professor Otto, appears in "The Bone in My Throat," TS, Boston University Library.

10. "Saint in Cellophane." See also, Simonson, pp. 93–98.

11. J. Abelson, *Jewish Mysticism* (London: Macmillan & Co., 1913), p. 12.

12. These words were used by Yezierska's daughter to describe her attitude toward John Dewey. They seem equally apt here. See letter to Jo Ann Boydston, quoted in Boydsten, p. xl.

13. Boydsten, pp. xll–xlvi.

Chapter Six

1. N. L. Rothman, "Artist Unfrozen" (review of *Red Ribbon*), *Saturday Review of Literature,* 4 November 1950, p. 13.

2. Ferris Greenslet to Anzia Yezierska, 6 October 1943, Houghton Mifflin Records.

3. W. H. Auden, *The Dyer's Hand and Other Essays* (New York: Random House, 1962), pp. 327–34.

4. Yezierska to Auden, 7 March 1950, Scribner Letters.

5. 7 March 1950, Scribner Letters.

6. Orville Prescott, *New York Times*, 11 September 1950, p. 21.

7. Boydston, p. xliv.

8. Concerning these chapters, Yezierska wrote John Wheelock: "A whole section dealing with my attempt to get an education has been cut out. When I found myself at a standstill in writing, Zona Gale offered me a fellowship at Wisconsin University. I had a chance to observe Meiklejohn's Experimental College and had interesting encounters with students and faculty. But I cut all this out because I felt my criticism of American education wasn't ripe enough." 15 January 1950, Scribner Letters.

9. Prescott, p. 21.

10. *New York Times*, 24 September 1950, VI, p. 14.

11. Robert Langbaum, "Ambiguous Pilgrimage," *Commentary*, January 1951, pp. 104–106.

12. *Jewish Frontier*, March 1951, pp. 28–30.

13. Auden, p. 328.

14. Ibid., p. 334.

Chapter Seven

1. Yezierska to Wheelock, 15 January 1950. In her letter she said, "A better name for this course would be applied humanity, the history of man in search of himself."

2. Yezierska to Auden, 2 March 1950. Again, on 7 March, she wrote that "one page of simple, honest writing, one poem from the heart. . ." was what she had wanted him to write for the introduction to *Red Ribbon*.

3. Review of *The Gift and the Giver* by Cornelia Wright, *New York Times*, 22 December 1957, p. 14.

4. Review of *Some Love, Some Hunger* by Millen Brand, *New York Times*, 20 March 1955, p. 5.

5. Review of *The Forester* by Maria Kuncewiez, *New York Times*, 12 September 1954, p. 31.

6. Review of *The Gift and the Giver*.

7. Review of *Gimpel the Fool and Other Stories* by Isaac Bashevis Singer, *New York Times*, 29 December 1957, p. 4.

8. Review of *The Landsman* by Peter Martin, *New York Times*, 10 August 1952, p. 4.

9. Review of *Cowboy on a Wooden Horse* by Yuri Suhl, *New York Times*, 25 October 1953, p. 4.

10. Reviews of *My Promised Land* by Molly Lyons Bar David, 29 November 1953, p. 18; *The Spark and the Exodus* by Benedict and Nancy Friedman, 13 June 1954, p. 22; *New Face in the Mirror* by Yael Dayan, 16 August 1959, p. 4. All from *New York Times*.

11. Review of *The Gift and the Giver,* p. 14.

12. Review of *New Face in the Mirror,* p. 4.

13. Review of *Tower of Ivory* by Rudolfe L. Fonseca, *New York Times*, 12 April 1954, p. 4.

14. Review of *My Promised Land,* p. 18.

15. Audrey Urbanezyk, "Old Age Can Be Start of New Life," *Journal and Courier* (Lafayette, Indiana), 15 May 1965, p. 12.

16. Letters of 13 February 1962 and 21 January 1965. Louise Henriksen supplied the information that Professor Leon Edel was responsible for these stipends.

17. Louise Henriksen kindly permitted me to listen to this tape, which is in her possession.

18. "The Lower Depths of Upper Broadway," *Reporter*, 19 January 1954, pp. 26–29.

19. "A Chair in Heaven," *Commentary*, December 1956, pp. 550–57.

20. "One Thousand Pages of Research," *Commentary*, July 1963, pp. 60–65.

21. An article, focused on Yezierska's participation, appeared in *Time*, 20 January 1964, p. 77.

22. "A Window Full of Sky," *Reporter*, 2 July 1964, pp. 29–31.

23. "Take Up Your Bed and Walk," *Chicago Jewish Forum*, Spring 1969, pp. 162–66.

24. *The Open Cage,* ed. Alice Kessler-Harris (New York, Persea Books 1979).

25. Boston University Collection.

26. Louise Henriksen Papers.

27. *New York Times*, 23 November 1970, p. 40.

Selected Bibliography

Manuscripts of Anzia Yezierska's published and unpublished writings can be found in the Boston University Library or in the possession of her daughter, Louise Levitas Henriksen.

PRIMARY SOURCES

Hungry Hearts. Boston: Houghton Mifflin Company, 1920.
Salome of the Tenements. New York: Boni and Liveright, 1923.
Children of Loneliness. New York: Funk and Wagnalls, 1923.
Breadgivers. Garden City, N. Y.: Doubleday, Page & Company, 1925.
Arrogant Beggar. Garden City, N. Y.: Doubleday, Page & Company, 1927.
All I Could Never Be. New York: Brewer, Warren and Putnam, 1932.
Red Ribbon on a White Horse. New York: Charles Scribner's Sons, 1950.
"The Lower Depths of Upper Broadway." *Reporter,* 19 January 1954, pp. 26–29.
"A Chair in Heaven." *Commentary,* December 1956, pp. 550–75.
"One Thousand Pages of Research."*Commentary,* July 1963, pp. 60–65.
"A Window Full of Sky." *Reporter,* 2 July 1964, pp. 29–31.
"Take Up Your Bed and Walk," *Chicago Jewish Forum,* Spring 1969, pp. 162–66.
The Open Cage: An Anzia Yezierska Collection. Selected by Alice Kessler-Harris. New York: Persea Books, 1979.

SECONDARY SOURCES

1. Books

Angoff, Charles. "Jewish Literature in English." In *Jewish Life in America.* Edited by T. Friedman and Robert Gordis. New York: Thomas Yoseloff, 1955, pp. 197–209. Survey of Yezierska's novels and her place among American Jewish writers.

Baum, Charlotte; Hyman, Paula, and Michel, Sonya. *The Jewish Woman in America*. New York: The Dial Press, 1976. Thoughtful study covering women's theological, cultural and economic status.

Boydston, Jo Ann. "Introduction" to her edition of *The Poems of John Dewey*. Carbondale: Southern Illinois University Press, 1977, pp. ix–lxvii. Definitive account of the relationship of John Dewey and Anzia Yezierska.

Handlin, Oscar. *Adventure in Freedom*. Port Washington, N. Y.: Kennikat, 1971. Good survey of American Jewish history.

Hapgood, Hutchins. *The Spirit of the Ghetto: Studies of the Jewish Quarter of New York*. 1902; rpt. Cambridge: Harvard University Press, 1965.

Harris, Alice Kessler. "Introduction" to *Breadgivers*. Rpt. New York: Persea, 1976. One of the first to "rediscover" Yezierska's fiction.

Hart, Henry. *Dr. Barnes of Merion*. New York: Farrar, Straus and Co., 1963. An account of Yezierska's involvement in John Dewey's seminars and research project in Philadelphia.

Howe, Irving. *The World of Our Fathers*. New York: Harcourt, Brace Jovanovich, 1978. Interesting analysis of the Lower East Side, although inaccurate on Yezierska.

Liptzin, Sol. *The Jew in American Literature*. New York: 1966. Brief discussion of Yezierska in historical context.

O'Brien, Edward J. *The Advance of the Short Story*. New York: Dodd Mead and Co., 1923. The man who awarded Yezierska the prize for the best short story of 1918 analyzes her faults and virtues as a short story writer.

Rischin, Moses. *The Promised City: New York's Jews. 1870–1914*. New York: Harper and Row, 1962. Thorough survey of the growth of the East Side community.

Sanders, Ronald. *The Downtown Jews*. New York: New American Library, 1969. Study of East European immigrants, focusing on Socialist movement.

Zberowski, Mark, and Herzog, Elizabeth. *Life Is with People*. New York: Schocken Books, 1952. A loving recreation of the traditions of the East European Jewish villages.

2. Periodicals

Brody, Alter. "Yiddish in American Fiction." *American Mercury,* February 1926, pp. 205–207. Critical assessment of Yezierska's use of dialect.

Browne, Edythe H. "A Hungry Heart." *Bookman,* September 1923–February 1924, pp. 269–71. An early interview.

Eisele, J. Christopher. "John Dewey and the Immigrants." *History of Education Quarterly.* Spring 1975, pp. 67–75. Consideration of Dewey's position on assimilation.

Gaer, Yossif. "Her One Virtue." *Menorah Journal,* February 1926, pp. 205–208. Critical discussion of Yezierska's portraits of immigrant Jews.

Goodman, Henry. "What Anzia Yezierska Doesn't Know About East Side Fills Two Books." *Forward,* 25 November 1923, English Page. Provocative review of *Salome* and *Children of Loneliness.*

Hindus, Milton. "The Art of Anzia Yezierska." *Chicago Jewish Forum,* Winter 1966–67, pp. 136–41. Sympathetic survey of Yezierska's works.

Langbaum, Robert. "Ambiguous Pilgrim." *Commentary,* January 1951, pp. 104–106. Thoughtful review of *Red Ribbon.*

Phelps, William Lyons. "How the Other Half Lives." *Literary Digest International Book Review,* December 1923, pp. 21, 94. An early booster of Yezierska whose articles show how the myths about her were perpetuated.

————. "The Heroine as a Woman of Letters." *Literary Digest International Review of Books,* October 1925, pp. 24, 719.

Popkin, Zelda F. "A New Adventure in the Promised Land." *American Hebrew,* 3 December 1920, pp. 112–13. An early review providing the viewpoint of the more assimilated Jewish community.

Roberts, W. Adolphe. "My Ambitions at 21 and What Became of Them—III Anzia Yezierska." *American Hebrew,* 25 August 1922, pp. 342, 358. An early interview.

3. Dissertations

Gartner, Carol Blicker. "A New Mirror for America: The Fiction of the Immigrant of the Ghetto, 1870–1930." Diss. New York University, 1970. Incisive analysis of Yezierska's early fiction.

Gordon, Nicholas Karl. "Jewish and American: A Critical Study of the Fiction of Cahan, Yezierska, Frank and Lewisohn." Diss. Stanford University, 1968. Interesting comparison of Yezierska's works with other Jewish-American writers.

Greenberg, Abraham Herbert. "The Ethnocentric Attitude of Some Jewish-American Writers: Educational Implications." Diss. Yeshiva University, 1956. Valuable for report of an interview with Yezierska during her later years.

Neidle, Ceeyle S. "The Foreign Born View America: A Study of Autobiographies Written by Immigrants to the United States." Diss. New York University, 1962. Although viewing Yezierska's work as autobiography, it provides some valuable insights.

Index